DAVID W. LATKO

Financial
Strategies for
Today's Widow

Coping with the Economic
Challenges of Losing a Spouse

A Fireside Book / Published by Simon & Schuster / New York London Toronto Sydney Singapore

FIRESIDE
Rockefeller Center
1230 Avenue of the Americas
New York, NY 10020

For information about special discounts for bulk purchases,
please contact Simon & Schuster Special Sales:
1-800-456-6798 or business@simonandschuster.com

Designed by William P. Ruoto

Manufactured in the United States of America

1   3   5   7   9   10   8   6   4   2

Library of Congress Cataloging-in-Publication Data
Latko, David W.
Financial strategies for today's widow : coping with the economic
challenges of losing a spouse / David W. Latko.
        p.   cm.
     1. Widows—Finance, Personal.   I. Title.
            HG179.L325   2003
     332.024'0654—dc21   2003042718

ISBN 0-7432-4373-0

*For my wife, Jan, without whose love,
support, and encouragement I would not
know how to go on; and for my two
children, Tiffany and David, Jr., whose
happiness, well-being, and future are my
greatest pleasure.*

Contents

Acknowledgments ix

Introduction 1

1 "So What Should I Do—*Right Now?*" 7

2 "...And Then the Sharks Began to Circle..." 13

3 Planning for His Passing 25

4 Picking the Right Financial Advisor:
Six Questions to Ask 56

5 "Greetings, Madam Tycoon!"
(Or, the Games Brokers Play) 62

6   "But I'm Too Young to Be a Widow!"   92

7   The Second Time Around: The Joy of Prenuptials   114

8   Making Sure There Will Always Be Enough   125

9   Passing It Along (Or "Being of Sound Mind . . . ")   169

10   Housing, Credit, and the Joys of Day-to-Day Living   186

11   A Taxing Problem: The IRS and You   230

12   The World of Scams and Con Games:
     A Primer for Widows Everywhere   240

     Afterword: The First Day of the Rest of Your Life   269

     Glossary of Financial and Investment Terminology   273

     Index   292

Acknowledgments

This book is the product of the life experiences of many people, the majority of them my clients for twenty years or longer, and all of them my friends; I thank each of them for the trust they have placed in me.

I also want to thank Joelle Delbourgo, my agent, for her tireless efforts and the courage and faith she placed in my abilities. I respect her, and hopefully, with her support and great talents, this book will be the first of many.

A huge thank you to Earl Merkel for his suggestions throughout the conception and development of this book. In the beginning of this project he was a business associate who only shared my vision. In the end I now consider him among my closest personal friends.

Thanks to everyone on my staff, who was always there to pick up the slack in the office during all those twenty-six hour days I put in on this project. This courtesy allowed me the luxury of daring to believe this book could become a reality.

My warmest appreciation to Gary Russell, my Iowa connection, whose encouragement, friendship, and daily laughter made this journey enjoyable.

Kudos also to all the great people behind the scenes at Simon & Schuster, including Doris Cooper, my editor, and Nicole Diamond, the acquiring editor, for leading the way and for taking my final effort to yet another level.

And of course a big thank you to my father, John J. Latko, and my deceased mother, Violet Latko, for giving me the values, drive, and tools to succeed in life and the encouragement to always follow my dreams. Thanks also to my stepmother, Genevieve Latko, for her concern and for trying to make our family part of her own.

To my older and only brother, John A. Latko, thanks for letting me tag along for all those years when we were kids. Thanks for your brotherly guidance and all the love you have inside for me and for all of my family.

Finally, to God, for the strength and courage to always do "the right thing."

As they say, "That's all, folks."

David

Introduction

Not too long ago, a very nice lady named Marianne* and I had a cup of coffee in my office. Marianne is one of my favorite success stories and has been one of my clients long enough to feel comfortable talking about herself.

"The worst part was just before Peter died," Marianne said, matter-of-factly. "We both knew his illness was terminal, and I tried to keep up a brave front for his sake. During the day, I usually did all right—but at night, I would lie awake, staring at the ceiling. I would listen to his breathing, feeling that I should be thinking about him. But all the while I was wondering what would become of *me*. I was terrified."

Names of actual persons have been changed throughout this book.

And she is not alone.

The actuarial tables do not lie: On average, most women will outlive their husbands by as much as a decade and usually more. In fact, in the year 2000 the average age of a widow in the United States was slightly more than fifty-five years.

With an average life expectancy of more than seventy-five, that translates into a lot of years where a widowed woman must deal with the issues of her own well-being without her primary life partner's advice or guidance.

And, as the horrific events of September 11, 2001 so tragically illustrated, the potential for widowhood is not limited by age. While much of this book is aimed at the needs of the older widow, this book also deals with the unique needs of the younger widow. Today, it is not unusual for a woman in the prime of her life to find herself —and very possibly her young children—the survivors of what she had planned as a lifelong relationship.

Nor is it unusual for a widow of any age to find herself suddenly faced with a staggering number of questions and decisions to make about her financial situation.

Ask yourself: If this happened to you, would you be prepared?

Most of my women clients are like Marianne; they are intelligent, capable, and competent people. And most of them are also widows who spent the larger part of their adult life with their financial affairs managed by their husbands. It was a system that worked—until the "managing" partner suddenly was no longer there.

Here's a quick five-question quiz involving just a few of the areas we cover in this book. Do you:

- Know exactly what your assets are, where they are, and how to access them?
- Understand how to establish your own credit, in your own name, and know why this is important?
- Understand how to structure your finances to keep from losing a large part of your money each year to such expenses as excess taxes, hidden bank fees, commissions, inflation, or confidence artists who prey on the unwary?
- Know how to sell your home for the best price, buy a car without being bilked, obtain insurance—both long-term care and other—that provides the right coverage at the lowest possible cost to you?
- Know how to develop a financial plan that will allow you to live comfortably, without the worry that your money will run out before you die?

If you answered all of these questions in the affirmative, great! You probably don't need this book.

But in all likelihood, you probably do.

Let me tell you about another of my clients. I'll call her Connie. She's a great lady—intelligent, attractive, and a lively conversationalist who loves to show me photos of her four grandchildren. She visits us in the office regularly, usually with something she's baked especially for us, and she always brightens up the room.

These days, Connie is living a good life, and she knows it. She also knows it could so easily have been different. For Connie, one of the worst days of her life was also the day that she now recalls most fondly.

"My Roger had died suddenly, in an auto accident," she remembers. "I was in such a state of shock. And then, at the funeral this person came up and just knelt by my chair. He took my hand and said, 'Connie, don't fear for anything. You are well taken care of.' It was what I needed to know at that moment—I couldn't stop thinking about what would become of me and begin the process of mourning. Those words helped me begin to put Roger to rest."

I happened to hear Connie telling that story a few months ago, and it left me feeling proud—and more than a little bit sad, too.

Proud, because I was the person who knelt beside her on that terrible afternoon almost a decade earlier; proud too, because I had the ability to tell this good woman something that helped her get through her pain and sorrow.

But the sadness I felt came from the knowledge that there are thousands of women out there just like Connie, women who, through no fault of their own, suddenly find themselves without their life partner, their mate, their best friend—and, more often than not, their financial mainstay, chief decision maker, and manager of their life security. And when that happens, even if they are surrounded by loving family and friends, they truly know the meaning of being on their own.

I overheard Connie's story late one afternoon and couldn't get it out of my mind. That night, I sat down to start this book. I hope it helps you.

Most widows are like Marianne and Connie, suddenly cast adrift in a chaotic and frightening world where peace of mind has become only a distant memory.

And if that describes *you,* then this book was definitely written with your situation in mind.

I have spent more than twenty years as a financial advisor and counselor. Over that period, I've managed millions of dollars in pension funds for small businesses, and tens of millions of dollars in investment portfolios for individuals of both great and modest means. I've weathered periods of staggering economic growth and periods of terrible economic downturn, each with their own sets of pitfalls and opportunities.

Most important, though, is the fact that I have helped hundreds of people—widows and others—build for themselves the financial security that lets them sleep at night.

It's not magic; it's not even rocket science. It is a logical, easy-to-follow program that helps bring you up to speed on what you need to know, what you need to do, and what you need to avoid. It's a road map to your financial independence and security—a plan that is designed to work for you for the rest of your life.

It works for Marianne, and—if you follow the plan—it will work for you.

Are you ready? Then let's begin.

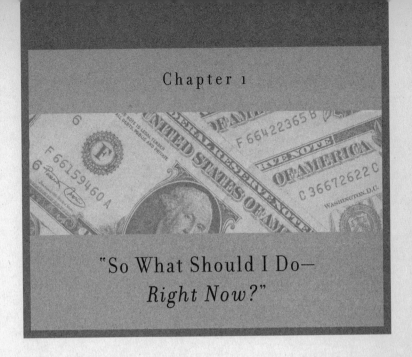

Chapter 1

"So What Should I Do—
Right Now?"

You are a widow or are about to become one. The decisions that were once the responsibility of your spouse have landed on your shoulders. You're probably fielding a lot of phone calls on subjects you know almost nothing about; your mailbox is probably full of bills to be paid and forms to be filled out; you're getting solicitations from people you've never heard of, a stream of whom arrive unannounced on your doorstep or over the telephone a couple of times each day.

Without doubt, you're getting a lot of advice from friends and family, much of it contradictory. And just the other day, maybe your kids sat down with you for the kind of talk that usually begins with the words, "Mom, we've been talking about what you need to do now . . ."

In every way, there's a lot of stress and pressure on you.

So what should you do, *right now*? I'll suggest something in another page or two, and the answer will probably surprise you. But first, let me just agree with what you already know: *Everything in your life now has changed.*

There's a book that I enjoy tremendously. I've not only recommended it to my clients, but I went out and bought copies to send to them. It's *Who Moved My Cheese?*, entertainingly written by Dr. Spencer Johnson, and it's a modern fable about change in today's world. I wholeheartedly urge you to read it, too, because Dr. Johnson's tale is probably pretty applicable to the situation you now face.

I'll oversimplify his message here: "When things change, you must change too—or die."

It's all too human to cling to the past; after all, we *know* about the past, don't we? We know we did x, and y occurred. Maybe it wasn't a perfect life, but by and large we found it provided a level of comfort, or at least familiarity, to which we became accustomed. A behavioral psychologist might call this "conditioning," and it's one of the traits that helps laboratory rats (and people) develop the patterns that ensure food, shelter, companionship—all the elements of a predictable, stable life.

The problem is when conditions change radically in a fundamental way. Now the rules by which the very universe works have changed; old patterns no longer work. And unless *you* change, too—unless you break out of the conditioning that has shaped your life—the inevitable result is a downward spiral into a final crash. So *you* must change, in a range of radical and even fundamental ways.

Sound daunting? It doesn't have to be, and to see an

example, let's return to that earlier question: *What do you do, right now?*

Answer: probably nothing. Certainly, nothing major.

This is not to say that you're going to draw the curtains, unplug the telephone, and sit in a dark corner, no matter how appealing that concept might seem at the moment. But it *does* mean that you are in no position to make life decisions yet—not until you have equipped yourself with the information and resources we'll be talking about in later chapters.

I've developed a simple five-point program that will give you a basis for your immediate actions. But even more important, the five points will help you avoid the kinds of actions that will come back to haunt you down the road. Here they are:

Point 1: Stop and breathe.

Point 2: Define your needs and goals.

Point 3: Love your children, but don't turn your life over to them.

Point 4: Don't become consumed by the financial concerns you face.

Point 5: Prepare yourself intellectually and emotionally to *learn*.

Five points—I think you'll agree, not a lot to remember.

I won't tell you they will make the first three months— or the remaining years, possibly even decades—of your new life a bowl of cherries; if you're reading this book, you already know that does not reflect the reality of widowhood.

But the five points will make your life more bearable. Even more important, they will position you well for the new life upon which you have embarked.

To illustrate some of these points, in the next chapter I'm going to tell the story of Miranda. Like Connie, she also became a widow suddenly. But unlike Connie, Miranda found herself in a storm-tossed sea where every decision was hard. And usually, terribly wrong.

The Five-Point Program for Every Widow

Five-Point Program

Point 1. Stop and breathe.

1.   Take three months off from making *any* major decisions; you need time to think and recover.

2.   Make *minimum* payments on your bills. You can always pay them off later.

3.   *Do not* pay off your mortgage immediately. There may be better things to do with this money.

4.   Beware of con artists. Check and recheck all bills to make sure you owe them before paying.

5.   Put any insurance proceeds directly in a bank *money-market* fund (a safe investment account that still allows you to withdraw money as needed) not a long-term bank *certificate of deposit*. Avoid investing any new funds with *any* broker or insurance agent regardless of their pitch. There is rarely an investment that can't wait.

6.   Make sure you do not have more than $100,000 in any single bank. That is the maximum any single account is insured for under the Federal Depository Insurance Corporation (FDIC). Should your bank fail, anything over this limit is *your* loss.

Point 2. *Define your needs and goals.*

1.   Understand that you probably *don't* know much about investing and financial planning. This will change after you read this book.

2.   Understand there is help for your problems. I will show you how to find it.

3.   Start to think about your life plan, both short-term and long-term. This really is the first day of the rest of your life.

4.   Make a detailed list of all your concerns and questions about your new life. Make sure you write them all down and refer, revise, and add to this list often.

Point 3. *Love your children, but don't turn your life over to them.*

1.   Lean on your children (or other well-meaning relatives and friends) for *emotional* support, *not financial advice.* They can be great at the former, but are likely to be dismal at the latter.

2.   Do not give your children control over your finances. Children tend to be too aggressive or too conservative with their parents' money.

3.   Unless your son is Warren Buffett or Peter Lynch, tell him you will handle things with expert outside professional help. He may be hurt, but he will get over it.

Point 4. Don't become consumed by the financial concerns you face.

1.   Don't let fear paralyze you. It is counterproductive.

2.   Do not panic. Others have gone down this road before you—and survived. You can, too.

3.   Good answers are out there. Your problems can get solved with good financial and legal advice, and a little common sense.

Point 5. Prepare yourself intellectually and emotionally to learn.

1.   Accept that most of the rules of your past life have been erased. New rules will have to be learned.

2.   Accept that you are probably clueless and bewildered about your future; you must learn much in a short time simply to survive.

3.   You need to know how investment houses work, learn how to recognize the good advice and avoid the bad, and learn the basics of personal economics.

4.   You will need to break old habits and thought processes and develop new ones that reflect the world today.

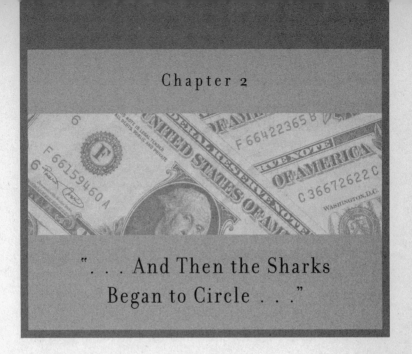

Chapter 2

" . . . And Then the Sharks Began to Circle . . ."

When Miranda first came to me, she had been a widow for almost eight months. Her husband Ron had been a regional executive for a mid-sized corporation; he had made a good living, providing a comfortable life for Miranda and their three children. After the youngest had graduated from college, Miranda and Ron had talked on and off about an early retirement and travel, counting on their savings, a modest investment portfolio, and the pension-plan benefits Ron had accumulated through his employment over the years.

Then Ron was diagnosed with a particularly aggressive form of bone cancer. Less than five months later, he was dead and Miranda was on her own.

"I was in a fog at the funeral," she recalled. "But that was almost a relief; it kept me from the panic I felt every time my mind cleared enough to think. Even in the hospital: Ron was dying, and I should have been thinking of him. But I couldn't help myself; the enormity of not knowing what would become of me would seize me. I would hyperventilate, cry hysterically. Sometimes I just sat in a chair, moaning. Really, just moaning. And not for Ron; for *me*."

It only got worse. Two days after the funeral, the calls began.

"When the first one came, I thought it was some kind of mistake," Miranda said, shaking her head. "It was someone from an investment house—a big name, one I recognized from television commercials. He said he wanted to offer condolences for my loss. And then he asked if I had considered my future security. I was speechless. He offered to advise me on investing, and without waiting for me to answer, started trying to sell me shares in a mutual fund!"

Miranda begged off from this first call; still, she would hear from this individual several times over the next two weeks.

By then, she had received almost two dozen similar solicitations from brokerage reps—none of whom she knew, but all of whom apparently knew how to read the obits and use the telephone directory to track down the recently widowed. It's a common sales tactic at major brokerage houses; it makes sense for these brokers, too. Obituaries give them a ready-made list of people who are confused, in need of direction—and who probably also have money from insurance or the inheritance.

And these weren't the only calls. As she discovered, a lot of people read the obituary pages. Not all of them are honest, or ethical.

"I had calls from real estate agents, wanting to know if I intended to sell our home, because they had people ready to buy it," Miranda said. "Most also had 'great deals' on condominiums, but I had to act fast. Fortunately, I still had enough sense left to know I was in no shape to act, fast or otherwise."

The mailbox began to fill each day. Along with materials from brokers and real estate agents, Miranda was fielding utility bills, credit card statements, invoices of all manner.

"Ron had handled most of our finances," Miranda admitted. "Once a month, he would write checks and mail them off. For the first two months, I tried to do the same thing."

The problem was, some of the bills she received didn't quite make sense. For instance, there was one addressed to Ron whose letterhead identified it as an electronics-repair service, enclosing a bill for a television repair. Miranda didn't recognize the company and didn't recall any broken TV sets. But, like most of the other unfamiliar bills that arrived, it was for a relatively small amount.

So Miranda sent the checks. And kept sending them.

Until, that is, the arrival of another bill—again, it had Ron's name on the statement—for a subscription to a golf magazine.

I shrugged. "A lot of people subscribe to golf magazines, Miranda," I said. "Everybody wants to improve their stroke, or learn to putt better."

"Ron played tennis," Miranda said, dryly. "He *hated* golf."

For the first time in her new life, she had begun to notice the fins circling her in the water. There were, she realized, a surprising number of them.

About three months after Ron died, Miranda kept an appointment with a representative of the large, well-known insurance company that had carried a life policy on her husband.

"Everyone was very sympathetic, very helpful," she told me. "They reviewed the policy, showed me what 'final' papers to sign and where. And then they gave me a check for the full amount, and I thought the meeting was over."

It wasn't, of course.

She was courteously escorted to another office, where an equally sympathetic company officer greeted her. They sat away from his desk, Miranda in a comfortable leather chair with a cup of very good coffee a secretary had served in a china cup. All the time, the insurance company officer was talking, talking, talking . . .

"It took me a while to understand that he was discussing the brokerage company that was part of his insurance company," Miranda said. "He was urging me to open an investment account with them. He simply did not want me to leave with the check I had just received."

"Let me guess," I said. "He wanted you to sign it over, back to them, immediately."

Miranda nodded—somewhat grimly.

And she might have signed where they told her—it *was* a major insurance company, she reminded me, and they had been so helpful—except that Miranda's recent experiences had changed her, if only a bit. Her first reaction was no longer to trust strangers (particularly persistent ones).

Finally, she left, more than a bit shaken—but she left with the check.

Later that day, she deposited it in her bank; the large balance now in her checking account raised her confidence somewhat.

That evening, Miranda's children—two sons and a daughter, all in their early to mid-twenties—met at her house for the weekly dinner that had become a routine since Ron's death. She had just started to tell them about her successful escape from the insurance company when James, her eldest, looked around the table and cleared his throat.

"Mom," he said, " we've been talking about what you should do now," and proceeded to tell her what her children had decided about her future.

She looked around the table at them, hesitating. It was tempting: Everything about the past three months had been so new and frightening, and fraught with perils which she doubted her ability to avoid. Her children were offering to look after her, and she knew she could trust them. And of course, Miranda had been looked after for a large part of her adult life.

Miranda loved James, loved all her children. And while they were adults now, they were, to her mind, still young. Was she ready to turn over her life, her future years, to their loving but inexpert care?

The next day, Miranda started asking her friends for the names of financial advisors. One of the names she wrote on that list was mine, and a few weeks later Miranda and I finally met.

At that first meeting, Miranda still showed the emotional bruises of her experiences. But she also showed something else: a steely resolve. She told me her story, including the events since her husband's death. Almost immediately after, she started by testing me.

"I know I made some mistakes, and almost made a lot more," she said. "What would you have told me to do differently?"

Here's what I answered, using our simple five-point program.

Point 1: Stop and Breathe

Despite what others may tell you, there is very little facing you that requires an immediate resolution. A good rule of thumb is to give yourself three months off from any major decision making.

Oh, you'll probably still pay some of the bills that come in—the ones that you understand *fully and completely.* Your utility bills and the mortgage probably fall into this category; credit cards and installment payments may well not. But the fact is that nobody will be throwing you out of your house, turning off your electricity, or repossessing the tool set your late husband charged to Visa—certainly, not for missing three monthly payments.

You'll want to protect your credit rating, of course. If you're really worried, I recommend paying only the minimum amount due on any credit card statements or other bills during this initial three-month period.

But do not immediately decide to pay off all your outstanding bills, even if you have the money at hand. For one thing, you may be paying money you do not owe.

A significant number of scam artists target new widows as easy prey. These despicable bottom feeders read the obituary columns faithfully, looking for fresh, unsuspecting meat to cheat. They know a lot of new widows are not yet schooled in the ways of a sometimes-hard world, and they flock to take advantage.

Remember the movie *Paper Moon*? In it, Ryan O'Neal played a con artist who would scan the obits carefully; then he would visit the widow with a "custom-inscribed Bible" the deceased had supposedly ordered for his wife. In most cases, the bereaved widow would pay the so-called amount due, none the wiser.

So for at least three months, keep *your* money out of *their* reach.

The insurance check Miranda received? If she had only put it in a bank money-market, or thirty-day short-term certificate of deposit (basically a debt instrument issued by banks and insured up to $100,000 by the government)—both simple transactions which can be done in a short visit to a bank—the money would have been safely tucked away. It would have been quietly earning a little interest while Miranda regained her balance, both emotionally and intellectually.

As Miranda discovered, virtually every insurance company is affiliated with an investment brokerage firm; the larger insurers own their own brokerages outright. No insurance company likes to pay out a claim. However, when they do, their own pain is alleviated somewhat if they can somehow get the money back into their hands—the quicker, the better.

It's in *their* interest to do so, of course—but it is probably not in *yours*. So don't get caught in their game, or anybody else's either.

So what is in your interest? That's what you use the three months—and this book—to discover.

Point 2: Define Your Needs and Goals

Your three-month hiatus isn't a vacation, of course. It's kind of a time-out from doing, but certainly not a holiday from thinking or planning.

From the onset, as a new widow you must understand that you do not know how much you don't know—not yet. For example, your primary question is probably one of time-versus-resources: Do you have enough capital/income to last the rest of your life?

We'll look at how to determine that in a later chapter, but you should know now that the answer depends on making intelligent decisions, and you need information before you can answer the question. Ditto for other areas: Should you sell your house? Buy or rent? Advertise for a roommate? Move in with the kids?

So many questions, so few answers—until you've defined what you need and what you ultimately want. Remember Miranda: If you act in haste, you will repent at leisure—possibly, for the rest of your life.

Point 3: Love Your Children,
But Don't Turn Your Life Over to Them

There is no greater comfort in times of bereavement than the love of a family. When a spouse and parent dies, the survivors often become the primary emotional support for one another. For a new widow, her children may be the people she needs simply to go on.

Fine; but consider this: As well-meaning as they might be, do you want to bet your future financial well-being on the kids? Unless your son happens to be Warren Buffett, the odds are good that anything he knows about investment, money management, or financial security came from rumor, hearsay, or simply somebody else.

We'll look at this problem in more detail later (see chapter 10, specifically the section on housing issues), but I'll tell you now: The situation is fraught with danger.

One of the most common mistakes comes when the children are given power over their widowed mother's finances. Mom puts the house in her son's name. Down the road, daughter-in-law files for divorce, and suddenly the property becomes a marital asset to be sold and divided. Or maybe Junior has a penchant for investing in the market. When times are good, fine; but then the economy dips, and the stocks that looked so good to Junior take a nosedive.

Remember: You've known your children all your life. Have they always made the right decisions for *themselves*? Why should their record get better if they're making the decisions for *you*?

Put another way: If Junior is so smart, why isn't *he* rich?

Point 4: Don't Become Consumed by the Financial Concerns You Face

This is, of course, easier said than done. You're on your own, maybe for the first time in decades. You're worried about money ("Will I be broke before I die?") and possibly unsure how you even go about managing the minutiae of paying bills, establishing credit in your own name, and so on.

Remember Miranda's tale: Fear is counterproductive. It can paralyze you, if you let it. Instead, know that help is available if you know where to find it and understand how to tell good advice from bad. We deal with that in this book (and if you can't wait, go ahead and take a quick look at chapter 4, "Picking the Right Financial Advisor: Six Questions to Ask").

But right now, all you have to do is not panic. Your situation is not unique; other widows have been where you are today, and they have kept their heads above the financial waters without drowning in their own anxieties.

You can, too.

Point 5: Prepare Yourself, Intellectually and Emotionally, to *Learn*

By the time any of us reached maturity, we had gone through a long and sometimes painful process of learning.

And after all, isn't that what our early life is supposed to be? Education—whether formal or of the "school of hard knocks" variety—is an accepted part of life from adolescence through the teen years and even into early adulthood.

Yet most of us believe that by the time we have reached our middle years, we have earned the right to more or less coast along on our store of accumulated wisdom. In many cases, we have been able to arrange our lives so as to minimize, if not eliminate, much of the unpleasant or the unfamiliar in our day-to-day life. We may start to think that we have a lock on how things are, and perhaps even secretly pity the clueless masses.

Until, unexpectedly, our own roof caves in on us.

There are no guarantees in this world. Unless we understand that, any calamitous change can paralyze our ability to cope. For you, as with all widows, most of the rules of your past life have been erased. In so many ways, you have suddenly rejoined the ranks of the bewildered.

The only way to survive is to learn the new rules, and how to play by them.

Poor Miranda. The only way to put a positive spin on her experience is to consider it tuition in the graduate-level school of hard knocks. But one major lesson for the rest of us is this: Tuition is only worth the money when you educate *yourself.*

You need to know a lot of facts: how investment houses work, how to recognize the good advice as well as avoid the bad, maybe even how to handle the basics of personal economics such as establishing your own credit or filing your own income tax forms. This is only the beginning; there's a lot you have to know.

And it's not easy.

Maybe you know one of those people who grew up in the shadow of the Great Depression; maybe you're one of them yourself. Those who survived those harsh years bear special scars on their psyches. Much of what they are today has its roots in the privation they endured. For instance, I have several such clients who, as a result of that terrible economic trauma, learned to be "envelope people." You probably know what I mean: Each week, when the paycheck was cashed, it was doled out into envelopes marked "house payment," "electric bill," "groceries," and so on.

It wasn't the most effective way to manage finances (I'm not a great proponent of having cash sit idle, rather than work for you), but it was a survival system they learned to trust. And, significantly, it was the one they felt comfortable using.

These days, it's hard to achieve financial security by being an "envelope person." But it's equally difficult if one clings to the practices that may have worked in the past but which now only drag you further into a financial sinkhole. You have to break old habits and thought processes and develop new ones that acknowledge the changes in your life and your world.

That's precisely what the five-point program in this book is intended to help you do. In the next chapter, let's take a look at how it works in practice.

Chapter 3

Planning for His Passing

When I ushered Bill and Jan into my office one February morning almost seven months ago, I settled them into the pair of comfortable chairs in front of my desk. It's an office custom to offer our visitors refreshments, usually coffee or tea and maybe a few of the cookies some of our more domestic-minded clients frequently drop off at my office.

"What would you like?" I asked them.

I was not prepared for the answer I received.

"How about another year or two?" Bill growled, though his expression was genial. "The doctors tell me I'll be dead in three months."

I looked at Jan, who sat stiffly at his side, then back to Bill's face. It was one of the few times in my life I was speechless. Not that it mattered; at our first meeting, Bill did most of the talking.

Bill was a rugged-looking man—maybe about five feet, ten inches tall, with a pensive aspect to his expression. He was perhaps thirty-five pounds over his fighting weight, yet it was obvious that he was strong. At sixty-eight, the story of his life was written on his face: You could see that he was accustomed to being in control. He was the kind of man who wore the pants in the family when it came to finances and everything else.

Sometimes you look at the wife of a man like that and in her eyes you can see varying levels of anger or resentment. Not this time: Jan seemed very content to let her husband occupy the driver's seat. At sixty-three, she was slightly built, but it was obvious that exercise and personal fitness were important to her. Though she was outwardly calm, the recent strain showed only in the nervous movements of her hands whenever she forgot to keep them clenched tightly in her lap.

Bill was a man full of surprises. Almost aggressively, he told me that he was a working man who had never made more than $60,000 in his construction job in any given year.

"And I saved every damn penny, too," he said.

It was no exaggeration: They had a net worth of approximately $1.2 *million*. They had lived very frugally, raising their three children in a three-bedroom, two-bath ranch house. Throughout their lives, there had been no new cars, no bigger houses, no fancy vacations; any spare money was put away and saved. In just about every way, he was the embodiment of an adage that used to be popular in certain investment houses: Bill lived like few people *would*, presumably so one day he could live like few people *can*.

Still, Bill had learned early in life the value of a good

stock. He'd buy it, hold on to it, reinvest the dividends to buy more shares.

As we talked, I was struck by the way he spoke of his various investments: Some he spoke of in a gruff tone, his voice carrying a hint of disapproval, as if recalling some long-ago slight; others he spoke of almost fondly, a smile tugging at the corners of his mouth. He seemed to remember precisely when he bought each stock—this one he had earmarked for his then-infant kids' college fund, that one he inherited from his own father. He could even tick off on his fingers such milestones as when one issue split three-for-two or hit some other performance peak, much like another person might have mused over family vacations taken long before.

I half-expected him to pull out his wallet and show me snapshots of the stock certificates.

Now, in another sort of person, this kind of behavior might have been off-putting, maybe even disturbing. But not with Bill; he had a way of making it seem normal, almost endearing. Maybe it was the way Jan responded to her husband's stories, smiling when he turned to include her in his reminiscences and adding a brief recollection of her own that frequently made Bill smile in return.

In her own way, as it turned out, Jan was just as frugal as her husband. Though she had never held steady employment, Jan was a volunteer at their church and occasionally worked odd jobs. Her real career was raising the couple's three kids. She had been very happy over her thirty-six-year marriage to let Bill handle the financial affairs. She did not care about the investments or the net worth; she cared about Bill.

Jan faced a frightening future. She was in excellent health. There was every indication that she could live well into her nineties—but most likely alone, as a widow. Statistically, most women widowed in their sixties or later do not remarry.

Fortunately, there was no question of whether Jan could afford to live to a ripe old age comfortably. The question was whether she wanted to go on for another twenty or thirty years, given the tragic news she just received. Looking at her as she watched her husband's face, I wasn't sure she did.

Bill's voice cut through my thoughts, and I asked him to repeat what he had said.

"I said, I own twenty-eight different stocks and nine different mutual funds," he repeated, his deep voice firm and steady. "I bought 'em myself, and I manage 'em myself. But Jan won't be able to do it, so we need somebody to help her when I'm gone."

No wonder, I thought. Just with this part of the portfolio, Bill received thirty-seven different reports and tax statements at the end of each year: one for each investment he owned. And this didn't even include all the various quarterly reports and the odds-and-ends junk mail every investor regularly finds in the mailbox. Simply pulling them together to file taxes had to be a task that would have strained a veteran CPA.

I also noted that many of the mutual funds they had were invested in high-yield municipal bonds, which did not make a lot of sense for them. First, Bill had made it quite clear that he didn't want to keep what he called "junk" in the estate he would leave to Jan. Well, a "high-yield bond" is usually just a term brokers use for what everybody else would call a "junk bond." An even more accurate term is "high-risk bond"—sometimes so risky that it cancels out the possibility of actually seeing the so-called high yield they promise.

Second, with the amount of income Bill had made in past years, it was highly debatable whether he even needed tax-free income in the first place. In most cases, a broker sells tax-free municipal bonds to a modest-income investor simply to make the commissions—in Bill's case, a commission of *five cents* on every dollar he placed in the fund!

Okay, you may be saying, it's just a nickel—except that on a $100,000 investment, *it comes to $5,000 in commissions alone.* This is a pretty high price to pay, and usually it's the result of a broker preying on a client's distaste of paying even one cent more in income tax. Nonetheless, Bill had bought them and kept them—and now we had to explain exactly what he had and how to deal with them.

Bill's portfolio was starting to look like an attic, crowded with dusty artifacts heaped in every corner by someone loath to throw *anything* away. And he still was not done. A smart investor, he did not risk all of his money in the stock market: Scattered among several banks, he also had about $700,000 in certificates of deposit. While keeping that much in CDs is a questionable move, at least the money was there and available to Jan, generating about $28,000 in interest income. Add to that a very good pension from the construction union, about $38,000 a year. Social Security added another $13,000.

All told, they had an annual income of around $85,000, although they spent only about $40,000 a year. But the sheer complexity of their finances would have staggered even a professional, let alone a bereaved widow.

"Okay," Bill said, taking a deep breath and looking hard into my eyes. "Can you help us?"

Perhaps for the first time in his life, Bill was ready to listen to new ideas. Just as Bill had been so protective over the years, even in the last months of his life, he would protect his wife until his last breath.

We went to work.

One of the first things I wanted to do with Jan was make sure that she understood that, if properly invested and managed, there would be enough money to carry her on through her lifetime. In her case, the financial situation was what most people would consider very comfortable. She was also fortunate in that Bill was still alive, available to help her sort through the questions and issues that she would soon have to face without him.

Now, everybody's situation differs. But a number of the steps I recommended are of value to anyone in Bill and Jan's situation. Here's what I told them:

- *Be ready to relinquish direct control; be open to ideas that are different from your own*

  Years ago, Bill had adopted an investment philosophy: Buy a stock, hang on to it, and reinvest the dividends to buy more shares. Years ago you generally could not run this type of system through a brokerage house. You would actually have to buy the stock, take physical possession of the stock certificate (or have it held by the stock company's transfer agent), sign a form that directs the company to reinvest all the dividends into more shares of that stock, and monitor the statements thereafter.

Today, more than half of the "big" stocks traded can actually be held in the brokerage account, and the client can sign the form for automatic dividend reinvestment. The major advantage here is that you get just one statement at year's-end for *all* the stocks involved, instead of a bushel basket full of account information.

Bill had done it the old way—in large part, I'm sure, because he loved holding the stock certificates in his hands. As a result, he had purchased twenty-eight different stocks this way, which meant twenty-eight different reports at the end of the year he needed for filing income taxes. In much the same way, Bill had purchased nine different mutual funds. More statements, more complexity to manage. Finally, there were the CDs. Because of the $100,000 limit at the bank, Bill had split his money evenly with accounts at just about every bank in his town (and some out-of-town banks, too). The result: *another* eleven statements, all from different banks.

In total, they were looking at forty-eight different statements coming in every year. And this did not include all the additional mailings—you know, the ones you open because you think they probably mean something important about your money, but which are incomprehensible without a Philadelphia lawyer standing at your shoulder.

Well, Bill had read them all; I suspect he even enjoyed it.

He had established a life pattern wherein he personally managed what was by any definition a complicated financial picture. He did it flying by the seat of his pants. And through tenacity and sheer willpower, he had done it fairly well.

But the fact was that Jan was not Bill. Quite simply, Jan was neither equipped nor inclined to the task. She was completely incapable of dealing with an estate as complex as the one Bill had developed and managed, and both of them knew it.

Fortunately, when I detailed the complicated structure of their finances to them, both Bill and Jan were ready to listen to anything that made sense. That made it a much more straightforward effort for all three of us.

- *Simplify, simplify, simplify: Streamline your life*

One of the first things I recommended to Bill and Jan was they had to simplify their financial life. For instance, we had to narrow the number of holdings down—as a priority, getting rid of all the "junk," then start to focus on the sheer complexity of the rest—and quickly.

First we looked at the twenty-eight different stocks. After checking out the performance reports and various recommendations on all of the stocks in his portfolio, it was very easy for me to recommend paring the portfolio down to only eleven stocks.

Did I say "easy"? Well, it might have been easy for me, as an impartial advisor, but for Bill, it was roughly comparable to the scene in the movie *Sophie's Choice,* when Meryl Streep has to decide which of her two children will be saved from the Nazis and which will be sacrificed.

We also took a look at timing, which can be an important factor in protecting the estate for the surviving spouse.

In their case, some of the stocks we earmarked for sale would be divested before Bill has passed away. Some of them would actually be sold off after he passed away, for certain tax reasons.

In the end, all eleven stocks will be put in a brand-new living trust account we created with an attorney's help. A living trust is an account that is overseen by a trustee who has power over distribution of the trust's assets. It's kind of like being the executor of a will, except that the person who set up the trust may still be living.

Among the benefits from this living trust account is the fact Jan would get only one complete tax statement at year's end instead of the mounds of paper Bill enjoyed. Where we could arrange it, the stocks that could be placed in dividend reinvestment were; the others were set up to pay a cash dividend directly into the account. As a bonus, Jan would even be able to write checks against this account to pay her bills.

And we didn't stop there.

With all the excess cash that would be coming into the account as a result of the immediate and future sales of the stocks, we decided to take a conservative approach: Those proceeds would not be used to buy other stocks at present. Why? In so doing, we gave Jan an approximate 70/30 split on her investments: 70 percent of her investable assets in safe, fixed-rate holdings, and only 30 percent in the stock market. That's a pretty good balance for anyone going through a lot of uncertainty in her life, and a very manageable split for someone with little personal investing experience. Best of all, we could always change these numbers in the future, as Jan's needs and experience changed.

The mutual funds were another story. Basically, we analyzed each one. We depend to a great degree on an independent rating company called Morningstar, which analyzes more than thirteen thousand different mutual funds to determine such concerns as their cost to do business, the commissions, the ongoing fees, asset allocation fit, track record, and much more. Even more important to us, what is their star rating compared to other mutual funds that are trying to achieve the same goals?

Mutual funds are ranked from five stars—the best performers—down to one star. We recommended getting rid of the one- and two-star (and even some of the three-star) funds.

- *Be prepared to look at the* complete *picture on each asset—particularly taxes*

In Bill and Jan's case, the four- and five-star mutual funds were keepers—*if* they did not contribute to the potential tax problems. Taxes can alter the wisdom of any investment radically and must be looked at very carefully. There are ways to minimize the tax impact, particularly when the death of one of the principals is imminent. Selected holdings can be given as gifts or as part of the estate, for example, to grandchildren. A good financial advisor will work with a tax expert to determine the best approach.

And everybody needs expert help in tax issues. Bill did not know about something that we recommend quite often: single-premium, tax-deferred annuities or variable annuities. These are contracts issued by life insurance companies that guarantee a specified fixed or variable payment at some future time, usually at retirement.

As I write this book, there are variable annuities out there that offer a 4 percent guaranteed interest rate on the fixed side. By the time you read this, the numbers probably will have changed, but the concept remains. These variable annuities are similar in structure to a bank CD. They give a yearly rate—sometimes a two-year rate, or maybe even lock your interest rate in for up to ten years at a time.

But the greater advantage is that they are tax-deferred, meaning that unless you take the money out during the year and spend it, you do not pay taxes on the interest it has earned every year.

Now, you can see how this might make a huge difference to them. At the time we worked with them, the interest rates being paid indicated that if the entire $700,000 in CDs was moved over in this way, that $28,000 a year that they were earning in CD interest would still be earned. The only difference would be that they would not be paying taxes on it until Jan started to make withdrawals. Since Jan would most likely be constantly rolling the money over—because she had no immediate use for it—this was an excellent strategy for her.

Remember: With a tax-deferred annuity, you get triple compounding, not just the double compounding offered on a bank CD. You get interest on your money, interest on your interest, *and* interest on the money you would normally have to pay the government each year. The latter is the bonus you get by keeping *your* money in *your* account, and not letting the U.S. Treasury keep it in its account.

The investments we put them in paid around 4 percent for the first year and had neither up-front charges nor surrender charges; Jan could take the money out any time she wanted it.

This saved over $7,000 a year in federal and state taxes alone just on this one change, as well as providing Jan with all the liquidity she could ever want. It gave her access to withdraw the money or to move it into an investment that offered an even higher return in the future. It would save Jan even more in future years, when she would start filing her tax return as a single person rather than the joint filing she and her husband had done.

If you consider doing likewise, remember three facts about annuities:

- Know that all annuities are not the same. Pick only those annuities that have top-of-the-line ratings from companies such as Standard and Poor's, A. M. Best, or Moody's *(see table on page 89)*. Because this money is not FDIC-insured, you want to buy an annuity from an insurance company that has the demonstrated ability to repay you.

- Always look for the annuities with the shortest length of surrender time. There is absolutely no reason to go with one that calls for a seven-, eight-, or even nine-year surrender charge; shorter alternatives are always available. And keep an eye on the broker you use for annuities: The longer the annuity surrender time he can talk you into, the more commission he will make.

- Withdrawals of earnings are subject to ordinary income tax and if taken prior to age 59½, a penalty may also apply.

- *Consider the advantages of setting up a revocable living trust.*

Very simply, a living trust is a revocable legal document that takes the place of (and expands) your last will and testament *(see accompanying discussion, pages 43–46)*. If set up correctly, in most cases a living trust achieves three things:

- It can help reduce estate taxes;
- It allows your estate to avoid probate, which is the judicial process where the will of a deceased person is presented to a court and an executor or administrator is appointed to carry out the will's instructions;
- It helps in cases where there is a disability involved.

It meant that when Bill could no longer manage his affairs (or perhaps even make a decision on his own), the living trust would give Jan the right to step in immediately and make those decisions for Bill. When that time came, there would be no lengthy courtroom battles or expensive lawyers.

Also, because of the size of their estate and because it was set up correctly, their trust could ultimately save more than $80,000 in estate taxes (depending, of course, on the year they died and the tax code that was in effect at that time).

There's a warning you should heed, if you decide to go the living trust route: Don't get fooled into buying complicated and elaborate trusts. Revocable living trusts can be as simple as a few pages or as long as a hundred. More pages don't always mean a better document: When I see the hundred-page variety, inevitably I find them jammed with filler pages that aren't important to the trust itself.

Sadly, unscrupulous attorneys exist; fatter documents mean fatter legal bills. A rule of thumb: Keep it short. And, depending on where you live, a good living trust (one that's not too complicated to prepare) should cost between $1,000 and $2,000.

- *Look into the self-protection of a million-dollar umbrella policy issued by a major insurance company*

For Bill and Jan, I recommended they obtain a million-dollar umbrella liability policy. This is something you buy through your insurance agent, and usually it is done with the same company that carries your other insurance coverages.

As the name implies, this kind of policy covers your liability up to $1 million in the event something really bad happens—say, an auto accident, or a guest slipping on your sidewalk. If a million-plus lawsuit comes along, the money no longer comes out of *your* pocket.

Let's say that Jan was driving home one day, preoccupied with thoughts of Bill's deteriorating condition, and failed to see a stop sign until it was too late. These days, even minor accidents often result in major personal-injury lawsuits.

I will not dwell on this sad possibility, except to say that you need not be an oracle to predict what a ruthless personal-injury lawyer could do in court. And you need not be a financial expert to envision the damage a liability judgment against her could have wreaked on Jan's future financial security. But with a million-dollar insurance umbrella over her, Jan could weather the experience without major hardship.

There were many other details that I recommended to Bill and Jan: how to save taxes, or how to set the estate up correctly; all the things that any savvy financial advisor can help do. The particulars of what we did are probably pretty interesting to financial professionals, though they're pretty boring for most other people. But *how* we did it is less important than the basic strategy we developed: simplify, simplify, simplify.

A great relief came over Bill and Jan as we finished up the appointment. You could see the trust in their eyes. Bill and Jan were very happy to have somebody show them that at least some answers existed for their situation.

As I write this, Bill is still alive, a testament perhaps to the same fierce doggedness with which he built the portfolio he and Jan had hoped would finance a long and enjoyable retirement together. But I don't see him much anymore. He's home from the hospital but far too weak to make the trip to my office. Instead, it's Jan who has begun to drop in, sometimes to discuss one or another question about her investments, sometimes just for a cup of coffee.

And we talk. Rather, Jan talks and I listen.

I listen to her talk about Bill, mainly: how he rallies on some days, enough to sit up in bed and talk. And I wonder about whether there is regret about the family trips never taken or the good times never had. People make choices, and the more astute of them understand that each decision brings its own ramification. Very soon, we all know without saying, Bill will be gone.

What will Jan have left?

The money, certainly. I can only wonder about the memories she has, or knows she has missed. We never discuss this, not yet. And Jan never stays very long on her visits, explaining she has to get home to take care of Bill.

When the end comes, Bill and Jan will be together. In their last months together—virtually in their last acts together—their focus has not been on the imminent ending of something precious. It has been spent with each still thinking of the other's welfare.

And in that, Bill and Jan will be secure, together forever.

I take a lot of pride in having helped make that happen.

Wills and Living Trusts: What Do You Need in Them?

Wills

A will is nothing more than a legal document that, if drawn up properly, will detail how you want all your possessions divided or disposed of when you die. What you put in that document is critical; careful planning will make all the difference. So what should your will include? Here's a short list of "must have" considerations.

1.   List all of your possessions separately and specifically who you want them to go to. Make sure you include all stocks,

bonds, bank accounts, brokerage accounts, automobiles, et cetera. It's also a good idea to list all your access codes for different accounts.

2.   Specify how you want your final expenses and debts to be paid. Are there certain things that you would wish to be sold first and others at a later point?

3.   If there are minor children involved, state who you want to serve as their guardian. Be *very* careful here. Pick a guardian who shares your lifestyle, values, and energy. Most of all, be sure he or she is capable of giving your children the love they need. It is a good idea to list several sets of alternate guardians, just in case your first choice is incapable (or unwilling) at the time you need them most. Always talk bluntly to prospective guardians *before* you name them in your will. Make sure they are up to this challenge. This is not an area where you want to take chances.

4.   Pick an executor and at least one backup executor in case the first one dies or refuses the job. This will be the person who executes all your final wishes and the probating of your will. You're asking him or her to do a hard, long, tedious job. Pick someone who is up to the task, has some financial sense, and doesn't live several thousand miles away. Remember to include some type of payment schedule for the executor. Don't expect him or her to work for months for nothing.

5.   It is important to name everyone you want to include in your will; it is just as important to specify those people you want to leave *out* of your will. For example, you might say something like "to my dear brother-in-law Jack I leave the total sum of five cents, and my best wishes." This will, one hopes, clearly explain to the probate judge your exact wishes for Jack should he ever consider contesting the will.

6.   Specify in your will whether you want a formal funeral, whether you want to be cremated, and where you want your remains to be laid to rest.

7.   Include a clause that requires the executor to contact (in writing) all heirs every sixty days; this can be a simple note stating what progress has been made to settle your estate. Why? One of the biggest complaints by heirs is that they feel left out and uninformed about when they are going to get their share of the inheritance. This should keep everyone happy—at least, for a little while.

8.   Don't forget those bequests to your alma mater, church, charity, friend, humane society, or any other entity you wish to include.

Bakers are good at baking; doctors are handy in medical situations.

If these facts seems self-evident, so will this one: Use a good lawyer to write your will. It will probably cost about $200 (though in many areas of the country, you can get it done for as little as $50). A good lawyer knows that sooner or later your will is going to come into play and that is where he will reap his big reward, a 2-percent to 8-percent fee based on the total estate value for his time to probate your will.

Keep your original will in a safe place, but where it will be accessible. If you have a safe at home, that's good. Safety deposit boxes in banks are bad, since upon your death the bank is legally required to freeze your accounts and other holdings— and that includes your safety deposit box. Make extra copies of your will and be sure they are available to key people.

Always keep your will up-to-date, if only because in life, things tend to change often. People win the lottery, remarry, divorce, adopt a child (or their children do), move to another state (different states have different laws), *ad infinitum.*

The biggest drawbacks of a will over a living trust is that:

1.   Wills can take a long, long time to probate (sometimes two years or more);

2.   Going through the process of probate is very expensive (the lawyer usually charges between 2 percent and 8 percent of the value of the estate);

3.   Your family has no privacy (anyone can walk down to the local courthouse and read your will); and

4.   Your family will lose control of the whole process (can't sell securities or get money out until courts and lawyers say so).

Also keep in mind that with a will, a court will take over your affairs when you become incapacitated. Why? What happened to your executor? Unfortunately, the executor only comes into play when you *die.* The court will step in when you become incapacitated to protect your assets until you get better or die, after which the executor finally gets involved.

Revocable Living Trusts

A trust is a legal document similar to a will except that in a revocable living trust, you place title of all your assets (stocks, bonds, real estate, bank accounts, autos, etc.) in the name of the trust for the benefit of your heirs.

Although a revocable living trust may look an awful lot like a will, there are some significant, important differences. Let's look at the players and elements involved in a revocable living trust.

There are four main players involved in a trust. The first, and arguably the most important, is the *grantor.* This is the person who actually creates the trust and puts assets in the trust.

Next is the *trustee;* you may have more than one of these. The trustee is the entity (usually a person, but sometimes an institution such as a bank or law firm) that will manage the trust. The trustee decides how to invest the assets, how to disburse them—in short, all the decisions that the owner of the assets would otherwise make, within the limitations spelled out in the trust document. Often, the grantor and the trustee are the same person.

The third player is called the *successor trustee.* This person (or entity) steps in for the original trustee(s) in the event he/she/it cannot or will not perform the job. This may be because of incapacitation; it may be that he/she/it just doesn't feel like handling the day-to-day affairs anymore. The main purpose of the successor trustee is to distribute your assets after your death, in accordance with your instructions. Frequently, the successor trustees are the adult children of the trustee, but the trustee can be a friend, relative, or institution. As with the executor of a will, you should always name two or three additional successor trustees, in case your first or second choices die or decline to serve.

The last player is the *beneficiary.* These are the people, charities, or organizations that will ultimately benefit from your death; they will receive the assets in your trust in accordance with your instructions.

There are several major benefits of a revocable living trust over a will. These include:

1. Your revocable living trust does not go through probate, so you avoid all the legal fees and the long payout times before your heirs get their money. This occurs because you actually signed over all your assets to the name of the trust; essentially, when you die you have no assets remaining in your name to probate. You will die, but your trust will "live" until you revoke it or until its assets are paid out after your death.

2. Because you have already appointed a successor trustee, in case of your incapacitation, the successor trustee will automatically step in to handle your affairs; the courts do not become involved. Again, this eliminates the associated legal fees and court costs.

3. If set up and funded correctly, a revocable living trust can actually help you to reduce or eliminate estate taxes in large estates (laws differ from state to state; see your tax advisor).

4. If you still have minor children, your revocable living trust can set up a special children's trust *inside* your living trust. When you die, the money you are leaving your minor children will not have to go through probate. (See your attorney for how to do this.)

5. If you own real estate in two or more states, a will would require probate rulings on those properties in each state. The legal fees and court costs can be high indeed, not to mention the time involved. With a revocable living trust you avoid probate entirely.

6. A major advantage of a trust over a will is in *how* you leave your assets. Let's say you have three children and an estate of $600,000. With a will, most people just divide all assets into thirds; after probate it is shared equally among the three children. However, should you want to make special provi-

sions—for instance, to specify that your "good" son gets his $200,000 up front, but the other two less stable children get their payments spread over the next twenty years—you can do this with far fewer problems using a revocable living trust.

7.   It is much more difficult to contest a living trust than it is a will. In today's world of contested wills and disgruntled (or disinherited) heirs, this can be a major advantage.

8.   A revocable living trust can be changed or discontinued at any time; all the proceeds can be put back in your name with little effort and expense.

With all the positives of a living trust, why don't more people set up living trusts instead of wills? Unfortunately, it comes down to money again. Most simple trusts will cost somewhere around $1,000 or so to set up, depending on where in the country you live; a will can be drawn up for $200, more or less.

Many lawyers will press you to go for the will, however. Why, if the cost is $800 less? He or she is thinking long-term: A smart lawyer knows that if he takes the $1,000 *now,* he may be turning down thousands upon thousands of dollars he could have earned from your estate if it has to go through the expensive, time-consuming probate process.

Trusts are almost always preferable to wills. The only exception would be in those cases where the estate is so small that it automatically bypasses probate (check your state's laws for the exact amounts).

While you're at it, ask your attorney or estate planner whether irrevocable trusts, charitable remainder trusts, asset protection trusts, personal residence trusts, land trusts, family limited partnerships, charitable lead trusts, or many other types of trusts could help your financial situation in estate planning.

And finally, *always* deal with an attorney whose main business is estate planning and who is experienced in setting up trusts. You'll most likely get a more informed and evenhanded opinion that fits your personal situation; in addition, you will also probably get the job done right the first time.

The subject of wills and trusts is important for widows to understand, both now as an heir to her spouse's property and later as a property owner who is planning her own estate. It's so critical that we cover it in detail not only here, but even expand on it later in this book. (If you can't wait, turn right now to chapter 9 for additional specific details.)

WORKSHEET:
PLANNING FOR A WILL

NAMES OF EXECUTORS (TO ADMINISTER THE ESTATE):

_____

NAMES OF GUARDIANS (AND ALTERNATES) OF MINOR CHILDREN (can have a Guardian over the child himself, and a Guardian over the child's property):

_____

PROVISIONS FOR PAYMENTS OF DEBTS AND TAXES:

_____

_____

SPECIFIC BEQUESTS OF MONEY AND TANGIBLE PROPERTY:

_____

NAME OF PERSON OR ORGANIZATION   AMOUNT OR ITEM

_____

_____

_____

DISPOSITION OF THE REMAINDER OF THE PROPERTY:

_____

NAMES OF PRIMARY BENEFICIARIES   PERCENTAGE
(INCLUDING TRUSTS):

_____

_____

_____

NAMES OF CONTINGENT BENEFICIARIES: PERCENTAGE

_____

_____

_____

Attach a list of assets and insurance policies.

Six Steps to Take If the Doctor Gives Your Spouse Six Months to Live

Step 1: Get Organized

Finding and organizing all the important documents you will need before your spouse dies will save countless hours and dollars later. Here's a list of "must have" documents you and your spouse should gather or note their location, as well as who to contact:

1. Last will and testament.
2. Living will.
3. Insurance policies: life, health, homeowners, auto, disability, nursing home, annuities, etc.
4. Copies of all single and joint bank accounts.
5. Copies of all brokerage accounts.
6. Copies of all retirement accounts: IRA, pension, 401k, 403-B, monthly checks.
7. Power of attorney.
8. Revocable and nonrevocable trusts.
9. Living trusts.
10. Titles to any real estate or automobiles in your spouse's name or joint tenancy and recent property tax bills.
11. Federal and state income tax returns for the last three years.
12. Marriage certificate. (In the case of multiple marriages, include copies of the prior relationships' marriage certificate and divorce decree.)

13. Birth certificate.

14. Medicare/Medicaid information.

15. Prepaid burial papers, cemetery deeds, burial requests.

16. Names, addresses, and telephone numbers of next of kin, clergy, doctor, lawyer, accountant, financial advisor(s), charities.

17. Safety deposit box keys and name, as well as address of box location.

18. The combination numbers and location of any safes you own.

19. Personal credit card statements to be paid and closed after your spouse's death.

20. Organ donor instructions.

Step 2: People to Listen to

Explain your situation, ask advice, and listen carefully to:

1. Your lawyer on setting up wills, trusts, and power of attorneys.

2. Your accountant on tax saving ideas before and after your spouse's death.

3. Your financial advisor on consolidating, selling, gifting, and beneficiary changes.

4. Your spiritual advisor.

On the other hand, don't listen to advice from well-meaning but uninformed sources. This may include children, neighbors, in-laws, or people you sit next to on the bus.

Step 3: Simplify, Simplify, Simplify

Things to do:

1. Clean out all the junk in the attic and basement. You never used it, and it's doubtful that anyone else will either. Sell, donate, or scrap it.

2. Consolidate bank accounts. Close out all those little accounts you opened to get the free toaster, can opener, or four-piece glass set. (Make sure you do not have over $100,000 in any single bank.)

3. Consolidate brokerage accounts into one account with the broker you trust most. If you don't have one, find one. (Make sure your account does not exceed the insured amount of the account.)

4. Have any monthly checks you receive switched to direct deposit.

5. Make sure you understand why your spouse divided the money between the above accounts.

6. Interview and decide on a financial advisor you can trust.

7. Throw out old statements and unneeded files. No one will need your telephone bills from 1947, a copy of your 1961 pay stubs, or the manual for your first color TV set.

Step 4: Get Your Spouse's Will in Shape; Consider the Advantages of a Revocable Living Trust

Living trusts can:

1. Possibly help reduce estate taxes;

2. Allow your estate to avoid costly and time-consuming probate;

51

3.   Help in cases where a disability might become involved and your spouse is incapacitated;

4.   Allow great flexibility and control in your assets;

5.   Be changed or completely revoked at any time during your life.

Don't forget to ask your attorney if an irrevocable trust would make any sense at this time of your life.

Step 5: Confirm Your Spouse Has Prepared a Valid Living Will and (at Least) a Durable Power of Attorney

What does a living will do?

1.   As a legal document, it lets you make the medical decisions—even if your spouse can't because of his medical situation. It clearly tells doctors, family members, and hospital staff what medical steps should, and should not, be taken.

2.   It keeps loved ones from having to make difficult life-and-death decisions on your behalf when they are most vulnerable.

3.   It lets your spouse decide if he wants to be hooked up to life-support systems or resuscitated when the monitor lines go flat.

4.   It lets your spouse decide if he wants to be kept alive or not by the use of feeding tubes.

5.   It lets your spouse request where he would like to die—at home, in a hospital, hospice, or nursing home.

6.   It lets your spouse state whom he wants and doesn't want at his bedside during the last days of his life.

7. It lets your spouse decide how much medication he is willing to take to make him comfortable.

8. The living will document can be changed or revoked at any time.

Note: Make sure the document meets all the requirements of your state law or it may be deemed void when you need it most.

A durable power of attorney will:

1. Appoint a person to act in your spouse's behalf in case he can no longer handle his own day-to-day decision making;

2. Make certain that this appointed person can sign checks, pay bills, buy or sell property, and basically handle your spouse's day-to-day financial affairs.

Warning: I would much rather see your spouse have a full-blown living trust than just a power of attorney. Why? Many financial institutions will not recognize *any* type of power of attorney; again, it's a matter of money. They don't want to be held liable for handing your spouse's money or securities over to someone else—even you—and then facing a lawsuit for doing so. They can't tell if your spouse changed his mind after he signed the power of attorney. Some may let your spouse have a power of attorney, but only if it is on *their* form. Check it out before you assume your spouse is covered.

Also, your spouse should be careful to whom he gives this power of attorney to handle his affairs. Miracles do happen. It would be disastrous to find that he regained consciousness and could go home and live a normal life only to find out that the person to whom he gave power of attorney skipped town with all his money. Again, this would be more difficult to do with a living trust in place.

Step 6: Review Your Life

1.   Help him to organize old pictures and write down relevant details (who is in the picture, when it was taken) for future generations to enjoy.

2.   Together, try to put together some type of genealogy report for your family.

3.   Assist him in writing letters to children and grandchildren to be opened at some later date telling them how he felt the day they were born, graduated college, or the most memorable thought he has of them and their lives.

4.   Have someone videotape your spouse talking about the highlights of his life. Ask him to tell stories that he wants people to remember him by.

5.   Help him write letters to old friends, detailing for them what they mean to him and why he valued their friendship.

6.   If it is possible, you and your spouse should consider taking a vacation with your children and/or grandchildren. The memories will be worth their weight in gold to them someday.

7.   Tell your spouse "I love you" twenty times a day.

8.   Help him make peace with himself . . . and do likewise for *yourself.*

WORKSHEET:
CURRENT INSURANCE POLICIES LIST

Life Insurance

Person Covered	Carrier	Policy Number	Face Value	Premium	Payment Frequency

Property and Liability Insurance

Property Covered	Carrier	Policy Number	Coverage	Premium	Payment Frequency

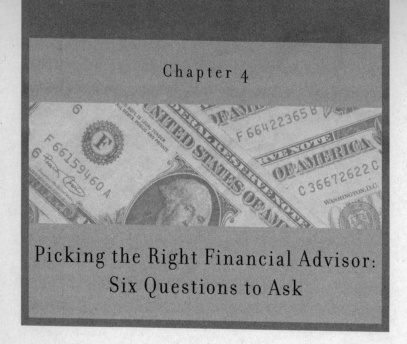

Chapter 4

Picking the Right Financial Advisor: Six Questions to Ask

Many people out there bill themselves as financial advisors. But advice can be anything but cheap, when it costs you money—whether in income missed through lost opportunities, by the outright loss of your capital through investments that were unwise or inappropriate for you, or even by practices that border on fraud.

So how do you pick a financial counselor who is right for *you*? Here's a list of a half-dozen basic questions to ask that will help you separate the wheat from the chaff:

1.   How long have you been a Series 7 registered broker?

A "Series 7" registration is the license required to sell stocks and bonds; an advisor who has held his or her Series 7 registration—and *actively practiced* in the business—for at least five years can be expected to be more savvy about the very information that you're looking to be advised about.

You're looking for somebody with experience—at least five years, and ten years or more is even better. More than 70 percent of "financial advisors" go out of business within three years of hanging their shingle, whether as an independent or as a broker at a major brokerage house. Moreover, such rookie "advisors" have not experienced the peaks and valleys that inevitably buffet the investment market. They are taught only one thing: how to sell what they are told to sell.

For instance, shortly after September 11, 2001, I had a flood of new clients contacting me, all in a panic. These folks were watching their portfolio value plummet toward disaster because they had been using bright young advisors who had never envisioned that the stock market could drop as well as rise. In their advisors' short careers, it had always gone up.

2. *What is the* minimum *investment you accept?*

The dollar amount here will vary—but the higher the number you hear, the better for you. A minimum of $100,000 or more is best. But certainly beware of any "advisor" who has a low-dollar minimum (or worse, *no* minimum requirement at all). A high minimum requirement tends to indicate an advisor is doing rather well and doesn't need to snare every walk-in simply to make the month's rent.

Don't worry, though, if your investment funds don't total in the six figures. Many people come to financial advisors without that much to invest. A good financial advisor will sometimes make an exception if you ask (but get a commitment that an exception won't mean a lower level of service). Others won't. One way around a high minimum is to hire an advisor who is licensed to charge an hourly fee. Be sure to check, because most advisors are not. If the advisor you *really* want won't budge on the minimum, ask about hourly consultation arrangements.

3.   *How many* current active households *do you have as clients? How many clients have you lost in the past five years?*

Two questions for the price of one! Let's take them in order. Ideally, the answer to the first question is between two hundred and four hundred households. Note: "households," not "accounts." One client could have a personal account, a joint husband/wife account, an IRA account, a pension plan account, a—well, you get the idea. Asking about "households" minimizes the opportunity for a prospective advisor to fudge this information. Less than two hundred households indicates a practice that is either new or probably not too successful; more than four hundred means you could easily get lost in the crowd. There are exceptions (for instance, fifty *very* large accounts could indicate a successful, established practice; a practice with a *very* large staff might indicate an ability to manage more than four hundred accounts well). But as a general rule, my numbers apply.

As to the lost-client question, the best answer is usually *not* "none." Sometimes, clients are "fired" by advisors because the client simply doesn't want to follow the advisor's advice or because the personalities just don't mesh. That said, the number you want to hear is "five," or even fewer. Generally, clients do not leave an advisor because of poor *performance*—markets have ups and downs that nobody can control. Rather, they leave because of poor *service*. A tip here: When you ask this question, closely watch the demeanor and body language of your prospective advisor; these may tell you more than the verbal answer you get.

4. *Have you, or your practice, ever had a written complaint filed against you?*

Ideally, the answer you want to hear is a strong "no." But in the real world, even good advisors can have a complaint on file with one or another of the agencies that regulate them. If your prospective advisor has had complaints filed, ask for the specifics of each circumstance. And ask about the specific outcome or resolution of each complaint. Certainly, though, if the number is more than two over the past five years, and the advisor can't provide understandable, believable, and overwhelming evidence that the fault is not his, politely excuse yourself and keep looking.

5. *Precisely what services can I expect from you? Will you handle my inquiries yourself or pass them to staff? Exactly how will you earn your money from me—commissions, percentage of my account balance, or hourly fee? How often will we see (and hear from) each other over the course of a year?*

You may think I'm cheating here, putting all these inquiries under the guise of being a single question, but I'm not. What you are essentially asking here is what *quality of service* to expect for your money. For instance, does this prospective advisor provide tax or legal services through their own sources? If you already have a lawyer or CPA you like, your financial advisor should have no problem working with them; if the advisor balks, it's a bad sign. But if you don't have these services already, it may be valuable to you to have the access to (or a reference for) legal and accounting services through your financial advisor. Certainly, done correctly it saves you time; it is also far better than flipping through the Yellow Pages playing *eenie, meenie, miney, moe.*

Similarly, you want to know what to expect when you call. Is your inquiry going to be bounced to a junior staff member rather than answered by "your" advisor? More precisely, if this happens, would it be satisfactory to you? Ditto for the compensation issue. You want to know the criteria for what you're paying an advisor, and the pros and cons of each method. An extremely good question to ask here: "Do you charge up-front commissions, why, and why would that be good for *me?*" Usually, you'll find out the answer to the latter part of the question is "it's not"; instead, it is very good for the *broker.*

And you definitely want to know how often you will get statements (at least quarterly; ideally, monthly) and how often (and under what circumstances) your advisor will review your overall financial picture with you (at least once a year, though an additional midyear review is often valuable). Ask about other contacts: For instance, many advisors publish a regular newsletter to keep clients up to date; others regularly contact clients by telephone to check in or alert them to opportunities or potential concerns. Still others prefer to conduct quarterly or semiannual seminars to bring their clients up to speed on the ever-changing financial environment and new investment ideas.

But practice varies; some advisors like to stay in frequent touch, and I'm one of them. For clients who provide me with an e-mail address, I make a practice of contacting them weekly with an update on the market.

The bottom line: The more choices they offer you to stay informed, the better.

6. *What makes me an ideal client for you? What don't you like about me?*

Taken together, these are good catchall questions with which to end the interview. In many cases, they elicit the answers that either cinch the deal or give everybody a last chance to politely walk away.

Listen closely to the answers and use your judgment. Be wary of the prospective advisor who has only good things to say about you or your financial situation. Stay away from advisors who pressure you to sign with them—*right now!*—without giving you a chance to consider your decision. A good advisor knows this is an important decision that may require time to make; he or she would rather have you take the time you need rather than encounter problems down the road.

Remember: You are considering a professional relationship that, in many ways, is similar to a financial marriage. A little honesty now—from both of the parties—goes a long way to helping ensure a trusting, mutually beneficial, and long-lasting future.

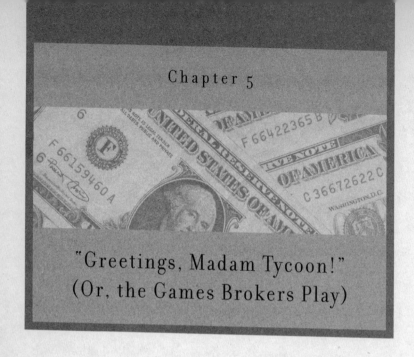

Chapter 5

"Greetings, Madam Tycoon!"
(Or, the Games Brokers Play)

"*Sell* it? Why on earth should I sell it?"

We were at the Q&A segment of one of the seminars I hold regularly in the Chicago area. Cynthia was still smiling at me, but I could see that her eyes were not quite as warm as they had been when we started to go over questions she had raised on her portfolio. In fact, they had turned down-right suspicious. They were the eyes of a woman who had been fooled before. I see that a lot among people who have been battered and bruised by what I call the Investment Merry-Go-Round.

Cynthia was a slender lady, perhaps five-eight or so. She was dressed impeccably. The jewelry she wore was equally impressive. According to the biography she had filled out for the seminar, Cynthia had been a widow for about two and a half years. She had no children, so throughout that period, she had been struggling through her finances—and all aspects of her life—largely on her own.

By her bearing when she arrived, it was quite obvious that she wanted the approval of the others. Later, when we had come to know each other better, I came to understand that Cynthia desperately needed people to think very well of her. If you're one of the many people who share this characteristic—and most of us do, to one degree or another—you understand how this can have an enormous effect on the decisions you make.

"You think I should *sell* it?" she repeated, as if I had advised her to set herself aflame.

I nodded, took a deep breath, and started to explain. Among other investments, I noted, Cynthia had been positioned in six different mutual funds. These had been bought over a dozen years or so by her late husband Bernie, through one of the country's largest investment brokerages. Cynthia's holdings appeared to be prudently spread in a number of areas—or so it would seem to the untrained eye.

The problem was that all of the funds were from the same family of funds. That means that all six funds in her portfolio were from the same mutual fund company. Red flags were waving wildly all over her portfolio, like red capes in a bullring.

Now, any given major investment company is going to have a substantial number of different mutual funds in its family of products. Large fund families such as Van Kampen, MFS, Franklin Templeton, and Oppenheimer each have more than eighty, for example. Fidelity alone has more than two hundred funds.

It's kind of mind-numbing, but keep in mind that, in

63

total, there are more than 13,000 different mutual funds out there from which to choose. That's more mutual funds than there are stocks on the New York Stock Exchange.

Some of them are stellar performers indeed, but not all. Some are riskier than others; some are too cyclical or focused on too specific a range of holdings; some just deal with income. A prudent broker will use asset allocation to spread out his client's investments, focusing on the best mutual funds offered by all the different investment companies in each of the different investment categories.

To put this into perspective, let's use an analogy. In any large city, there are a host of law firms you could consider for your legal advice; they all have strengths and weaknesses. Some have a great tax specialist on staff; another may have a great litigator, a real gunslinger you want if you sue somebody; a third is the world's expert on wills and inheritance law. Wouldn't it be nice to be able to pull together a "dream team"—the all-star individual lawyers from each of these firms? Well, with mutual funds you actually can; you can pick the best performer from Franklin Templeton, the best from Van Kampen, and so on.

Back to Cynthia: On the computer, I looked each fund up on our Morningstar listings. I compiled the combined performance; over the twelve years that she and Bernie held them, the initial investment of $25,000 had grown to slightly more than $49,000. Although this total return sounded respectable, in fact the average annual return was only about 6 percent.

Then I called up a couple of other investments in the same category that we usually use to see how they did over that same period. I could punch in a date and go back in time and see exactly what performance they had posted.

"Okay, now look at this," I said to Cynthia. "If you had put that $25,000 in these investments over that same time period, you would now have had somewhere in the area of . . . oh, $101,000 or so." That averaged out to a total return of more than 12 percent annually—and with no more risk than Cynthia's current investments.

Cynthia looked from the computer screen to my face, and back again. Her look spoke volumes.

Welcome to the Wild West, to No-Person's Land, to the realm where dog eats dog without remorse. This is the wonderful world of financial investment, where the wily wax fat on the carcasses of the innocent. Cynthia was just one more investor who had been terribly mistreated in the investments she had bought. How she came to this state is instructive for all of us.

Before he died, Cynthia's husband Bernie had set up pretty much all of their financial affairs; he had invested on his own, sometimes choosing wisely and sometimes not. Often, it seemed, his only guide was what he read in magazines or newspapers or heard from well-meaning but uninformed relatives and friends. When she inherited this portfolio, Cynthia had tried to make sense of it.

"That was a fiasco," she admitted. "I might as well have tried to read Chinese, for all the good that did me."

Failing that, she had gone to a branch office of a major brokerage firm and asked for help. The bright-faced young man there had a nice smile, she remembered, and sounded both concerned and competent. She remembered leaving the offices with a sense of profound relief.

Little did she know that what she almost certainly got was what is called "the broker of the day." This is the person who, when you come through the door of any major brokerage firm, is next in the batting order to handle walk-in prospects.

It's a crapshoot. You might get a broker who has been in the business for twenty years and who has only your best interests at heart. Then again, you might get one who was hired out of training school three months ago and whose former job was selling ladies' shoes. The interest this kind of person has is usually his own; he wants to sell you anything, as long as it brings him a big commission, helps him keep his job, and makes his manager happy.

Unless you ask about the broker's background and track record—and how could Cynthia have thought to do this?—you just don't know. Ask; a broker with nothing to hide is always willing to provide details.

Now, Cynthia had put limits on her new broker. There were certain mutual funds she owned that she prohibited him from selling, because those were the instructions left to her by the late Bernie.

While I'm usually not a fan of beyond-the-grave investment advice, in this case it turned out to be a good idea. When Cynthia saw her first statement, it came as a major shock. Despite what seemed to her a large number of trades—both buys and sells—her portfolio's value had not grown appreciably. In fact, because of all the broker's commissions, this time she was down almost 5 percent from her previous statement.

I scanned the statement again. From what I could see, Cynthia's former broker basically made a lot of transactions with only one clearly "positive" result: He made some pretty darned nice commissions for himself.

Certainly, nothing he did had helped Cynthia.

What this broker did was either completely inept or skirted what is called "churning the account"—a predatory practice that can (and should) land a broker in a hornet's nest of legal trouble. Now, I don't mean that changes weren't needed for Cynthia's account. But those changes should have benefited the client, not the broker.

After a time dealing with this sharpie, the situation became quite obvious even to Cynthia. She started looking—again—for better financial advice. As part of her search, she came to my financial seminar, where I had to tell her that her suspicions were highly justified.

Poor Cynthia. Poor *anybody* who looks for financial help without knowing just how hazardous the terrain can be. Picking a financial advisor can be tough. If you venture into this minefield, here are a few warning signs to ignore at your own peril:

Avoid Anybody Who Refuses to Speak Clear, Straightforward Language

It is essential that you understand everything you are hearing from a prospective broker or advisor. Force him or her to be clear and simple, and don't accept anything less.

For instance, let's say you ask a few questions and they seem to become annoyed (or even infuriated) with you. Or maybe they just give you that look—the one many of us remember from high school, the one that says, "How could you be so dumb?" It's a look meant to intimidate you, pure and simple. Maybe your advisor does not want you to ask those questions; maybe he just wants to discourage you from asking other questions; maybe he is afraid you'll find out he just doesn't know the answers.

If you are made to feel you are a bother to him, there's one thing to do: run. Find somebody else—someone who doesn't think that you, the customer, are an annoyance. You want a guy who makes you feel as if making money for you is the only reason he gets up in the morning. Jettison the broker who makes you feel any other way.

Avoid the "Aversion Therapy"-Style of Broker

Here's one of the more common tricks of the trade: When you call your broker with a question, he turns the tables on you. Instead of answering, he'll fire back question after question—each of them about *your* questions. In extreme cases, you may wonder if perhaps he wanted to be a psychiatrist instead of a broker.

A variation on this tactic: Every time you call, he'll pressure you to buy something—*anything;* there's always a hot new investment he's trying to sell you on.

Bottom line: Pretty soon, in either instance you avoid calling in. In the former, you don't want to feel you're being grilled by the Gestapo; in the latter, you just don't want the hassle of saying no to each new sales pitch. In essence, you stop "bothering" them.

They win, you lose.

Beware "The Contest"

If you could be a fly on the wall at virtually any brokerage house, it would be an eye-opening experience. Almost immediately, you'd realize that you're watching a group of experts at work; these people know about the art of making money. The problem is that much of their work is devoted to making money for themselves. That money has to come from someplace, and usually, it must come from you.

There always seems to be some kind of contest going on at any given brokerage house. Sound fun? Well, it can be—but generally, not for you, the customer. These contests are designed to loosen your purse strings. Here's how it works: The main office or region of a brokerage company picks the product-of-the-month. It could be an annuity, a limited partnership, a new stock issue, or any other investment that the firm wants to push.

One way to encourage brokers to get excited about pitching the product is to make it a contest: Whoever sells the most shares or units in a specified time frame (one day, one week, one month; it varies) may receive a bonus. The prize also varies: dinner for two, a watch, even an all-expenses-paid trip to the company's next exotic meeting location. Trust me, I'm not talking about a weekend in Minneapolis in January, either.

In fact, some brokerage firms will factor in the results in these contests when evaluating which broker gets promoted and which gets fired. They pit their own brokers against one another, the local office against those from other branch offices, region against region. Managers whip on their staffs, because a manager's year-end bonus is in part determined by such results.

All this isn't to make selling investment vehicles more fun. It's all about selling more and making more money—but for the brokerage house, *not* necessarily for the customer.

So ultimately, what can happen when the broker talks to you during contest time? Let's say there are two investments: The first is a sound one that is very suited to your investment needs and long-range strategy; the other is slightly less suitable, but acceptable enough—and it's the subject of this month's Calypso Getaway Contest.

Knowing human nature, which is he more likely to pitch to you? Even the most ethical and morally upright of brokers can crack under pressure—and by that I mean both the pressure of personal need as well as the pressure from the boss to whom he reports.

Understand That Some Investments Are Not for You

There are some sexy-sounding investments out there, some of which promise staggering profit potential. You may even have heard about some people who have cashed in big-time by "dabbling" in some of these vehicles.

But if you don't know what you are doing, these "high-potential" investment vehicles are better left to others. In most of them, you can easily lose what you invest; in a few of them, such as commodities, you are liable for losses over and above your initial investment. Unless you are one of the handful of people who know the ins and outs of the corn or soybean market, stay out of it.

In fact, I'm not sure it's appropriate for more than 4 or 5 percent of *all* investors; it's that risky. It ranks with gold fever, pitched by every gold bug out there who, when the latest global crisis "looms," urges you to load up on gold bullion or Krugerrands. Don't; leave it for the experts, who themselves get burned often enough in both gold and commodities.

Ditto for options. An option essentially is only the price you pay for the privilege of having the *option* to buy or sell a specific stock or market index, at a specific price sometime in the future. It is a bet, a wager that the stock is going to either increase or decrease in value dramatically in a defined period of time.

For example, let's say that IBM is at 100, and you think it will be 125 in the next three months. You have two choices: You can either buy the stock itself, *or* you might buy something called a "call" that gives you the right to buy 100 shares of IBM at—oh, let's say 110 any time in the next three months.

Let's also say that right costs you $4 per share: $400 simply for the right to buy 100 shares at $110 per share for the next ninety days. There is a potential advantage: In effect, it only costs you $400 to "control" that 100 shares, rather than the $10,000 you'd have to spend immediately to buy the block outright.

But now the clock is ticking: Your option expires in ninety days. So IBM must reach 114 in the next three months, just for you to break even. If it doesn't go that high, or if it drops instead—well, you get the sorry picture; you lose 100 percent of the $400 you put up.

Thus, avoid "call" investments (as well as their dark sister, the "put," where you're betting the stock will go down within a defined time span). This is not for the faint of heart.

Diversify, Diversify, Diversify: Avoid Proprietary Funds

I always look for big red flags when I'm analyzing a new customer's portfolio. One of the biggest and reddest of these flags comes when I see a customer whose investment fund management was handled exclusively by one of the major wire house brokerages, which is another term for a large national or international brokerage firm. You'd recognize the names; you see their ads all the time on TV.

In the most blatant red-flag form, these accounts own only funds that are managed by the wire house itself: for instance, former Merrill Lynch customers who own only Merrill Lynch funds, or Morgan Stanley clients who are invested in only Morgan Stanley funds, and so on.

Now, almost every wire house has good in-house funds, usually, at least one or two. But I've never known any wire house to have ten or fifteen good ones, and certainly none has the leading fund in each investment category. So why do brokerage houses like their brokers to sell just their name-brand funds? Simple: It keeps the money in the family.

Every mutual fund sold in the United States has something called "an internal management fee." This fee averages around 1.5 percent annually; if you have $10,000 in a fund, you pay about $150 for advertising, employee salaries and commissions, telephones, photocopier paper, and file cabinets—all the costs for running the fund come out of your pocket. A mutual fund that only breaks even for the year means you post a net loss of $150.

But win or lose, you'll still pay the fee each year.

Now multiply the management fee by the tens of millions of dollars invested in each fund, and you begin to understand the motivation for each brokerage firm to push their own mutual funds to investors. Now you can see why major brokerage houses love their brokers to sell their own brand mutual funds. Why send those lucrative annual fees (which they can use themselves) to a rival? It's the same with variable annuities, insurance, and similar investments.

There are other aspects of this game, too. For example, a brokerage house's proprietary products are almost always nontransferable. If your broker decides to take a job across the street (often, with a big up-front bonus of up to a year's salary) at a different brokerage, chances are that all those mutual funds you bought through his former employer will not transfer to his new job. He won't even be able to access information on any proprietary annuities or limited partnerships, either.

Your broker now suggests that you sell—cash out of what just a few months before he was touting as great long-term investments. Why? So you can move the money into "even better" investments, the ones offered, of course, by his *new* employer.

Sure, there will be a few associated costs: some big-bucks commissions on the new investments, any surrender charges that are required for cashing out of the old investments, maybe even some interesting tax complications. But, you are told, it will result in a "much better" portfolio somewhere down the road.

Meanwhile, the brokerage house that is losing you has assigned your account to a new guy. This is typically a high-pressure specialist who calls you twice daily to ridicule the logic of changing houses and investments. It's his job to keep you where you are, and he'll do almost anything to do so.

So there's a reason to worry about *anybody*—wire house *or* independent broker—who wants to load your portfolio with mutual funds or annuities that all come from the same company. He may be in bed with that particular family of funds because he gets paid a little bit more to push their products. Another possibility: The fund sponsor may have put a "bounty" on the investment, an offer to pay your broker a higher commission over a specified period of time. It's even possible that the wholesaler for the mutual fund company might be taking your advisor to dinner or a baseball game on a regular basis.

But whatever the reason, "keeping it in the family" is a definite red flag, and it is almost always bad news for your account. If your broker proposes such an approach, walk away and find a new broker, one whose primary responsibility is to *you*.

Pay Wisely for Advice

Essentially, there are three ways to pay somebody for the investment advice and management you receive: through an hourly fee, an annual percentage fee, or a commission.

For instance, let's say a person has $2 million, and she wants to invest heavily in bonds for monthly income. If she uses an advisor/broker who charges an annual percentage fee, that investment advisor will receive, say, 1 percent of her investment's value each year in payment for his advice.

Wow. Is it defensible to charge $20,000 a year—*every* year—for a fistful of bonds that she is going to own for fifteen years and probably never change? Most likely, no. Either a onetime flat commission, or a onetime fee based on how complicated the transaction was or how long the appointment took would be the most fair and reasonable payment for these services rendered.

Banks are infamous for this trick, though usually there's a slight twist. A bank may charge the same 1 percent annual management fee, but do nothing more than buy you "laddered" CDs (that is, CDs maturing on, say, a six-month basis, a one-year basis, an eighteen-month basis, and so on) issued by their own bank. They don't even bother to earn their money by finding you the highest-paying CDs available; they just pull their own off the shelf. They keep the "management" money, even when no management is provided.

However, if your advisor/broker is actively managing your portfolio—buying and selling, researching new potential investments, and so on—an hourly fee or an annual percentage fee would probably be equitable.

First decide which behavior you want to encourage: If you pay a commission for each buy or sell transaction, you are encouraging active buying and selling. This raises the possibility of abuse, usually in the "churning" of accounts.

With the advent of more independent registered investment advisors, alternatives now exist that did not only a few years ago. Independent advisors often can offer unbiased analysis because they have no corporate pressure to sell you the product of the month. Sadly, many brokerage houses and advisors tend to charge as much as the market—*their* market, of course—will bear; it is always going to be the highest price they can charge. Moreover, brokers have a tendency to get their commission money up front whenever possible, preferring a bird in the hand just in case the client decides to change her mind or move her account elsewhere.

But it is important to remember that somebody *always* pays, and that somebody is always going to be you, the investor.

For example, there are certain variable annuities out there that pay a broker 7 percent or more up-front—not directly by you, but by the company issuing an annuity. Sound like a good idea? Well, maybe: After all, it's not coming out of your pocket. What the heck—let the broker make as much as he can, as long as somebody else is paying, right?

Wrong. You may not *see* yourself paying that 7 percent, but the company that issues your annuity simply deducts that expense from what it could have paid you over the life of the investment if it did not have to pay your broker up-front. As a result, the company will usually include a substantial surrender charge in the transaction. If you sell in the next seven to ten years, it's going to cost you, big-time. Why? The insurance company cannot go back and collect the commission it already paid the broker; instead, it will get it back from you. Lower interest paid to you, large surrender fees if you want to move to something else, or both: One way or another the company makes back the 7 percent commission it paid to the broker.

It's not hard to avoid this trap. Today, there are variable annuities designed to pay the broker on an as-you-go basis. The broker still gets paid a fee each year for advising you on your investment, but you can cancel, cash out the annuity, and leave at any time without a penalty. For most investors, this makes a lot more sense.

Ah, you may ask, but what about "no-load" funds? These are investments that cost nothing to get into the game and nothing to get out.

The so-called conventional wisdom says "no-load" means "no-cost," but how could that be true? The half-page ad for the no-load in *The Wall Street Journal* costs upward of $50,000 just to run. It—and all the other costs of sales personnel, administration, management, and especially profit—has to come from somewhere. And it does: Once again, it comes from *you*.

No-load investments can be good for some people. These are usually the people with a lot of knowledge, experience, and both the time and the desire to manage their own portfolios. But I advise even these people to use extreme caution: No-load does not necessarily mean you'll get the highest and/or best returns. It may mean only you might be paying a lower annual expense charge.

We'll talk more about cost versus return later in the chapter. But right now, know that you must always look for funds that have a consistent, long-established track record of paying the highest overall total return. A low cost means nothing if you don't get the performance.

Paying an advisor on an hourly basis means that you "rent" the expertise when you need it, for as long as you need it. Particularly for people who take an active interest in their own investments, this can be the wisest and fairest course of action. Obviously, this can be a great advantage for such people; there's always an expert whose mind you can pick or whose hand you can hold when the market turns scary.

Unfortunately, today many advisors/brokers still prefer to work on commission. It has long been the custom in brokerage houses, though many have now started offering some fee-based rates (if only because more customers are demanding it). But if you have a reason to pay on a different basis, it never hurts to ask. Either party can respectfully decline if no agreement can be reached.

Always, Always, Always Know the Costs

It's incredible, but many people don't know the actual cost they pay for advice.

Unlike a gallon of milk, there is no price tag dangling from a financial advisor. Unless you ask, you're not going to find out until you get to the cash register, and sticker shock is rarely fun.

When you interview your prospective broker/advisor, ask how he operates his business. Is there a charge for this (first) appointment? Remember the different ways to buy these services; does he offer an hourly rate, a flat fee, a commission-based arrangement? If not, is his method the one you want to use?

When the broker proposes investments, ask if that investment is offered under an alternate type of commission or fee basis. Is the option of a shorter surrender charge available? Let him know that you don't mind paying fairly for his services, but that you are looking for a system that is in your best interest, not his.

If you are already a client (or if your deceased spouse was) and you are considering continuing the relationship, you'll want to sign a request-to-switch letter before you make any changes to a mutual fund or annuity. It's a matter of self-protection. A request-to-switch letter discloses to you all the costs of making changes in your portfolio and can prevent nasty surprises later.

These should be easy-to-understand documents, and constructed properly, they will let you know if you are paying any surrender charges on the old investment as well as if the new investment has up-front fees or new surrender charges. This is important, so if your broker/advisor doesn't offer a request-to-switch document, ask for one.

Make Sure Your Broker Protects *Both* of You

You need to know that whoever handles your investments is insured. Generally, this is done by SIPC (Securities Investor Protection Corporation) insurance, which is very similar to FDIC insurance. It works like this: All SIPC-covered accounts are insured by this government agency for a total of $500,000, of which $100,000 can be in cash. In addition, most broker-dealers and brokerages purchase additional private insurance on all their accounts; up to $100 million in coverage is not unusual. In this way, the broker actually protects you, while at the same time he protects himself and his reputation.

An important note: Understand that this type of insurance is *not* intended to cover any investment losses; it is there simply to protect you from extraordinary events. If, for instance, the clearing firm that is holding your assets goes belly-up, the insurance is your protection from ruin.

So ask if it is there, and how much there is of it. You do not want to just start giving out checks to people and then wondering if your assets are safe. And if your broker doesn't pass this test, definitely find someone else.

Beware of Looking *Only* at the Costs

While you must be aware of the total costs you are incurring, don't let the bottom line be your sole consideration. You're looking for value, and a dollar spent well is always a wise decision.

Remember that there are many different costs to consider. Let's examine some of the more important ones.

Mutual Funds

As I mentioned, every mutual fund carries an internal charge or fee structure. Some index funds that have become popular in recent years do not have a fund manager, per se, and as a result have low expenses of approximately .50 percent annually. Other funds with managers usually assess between 1 percent and 2.5 percent each year.

On occasion, I'll find a client who is so focused on that fee that she ignores other factors; she has been advised to pick investment funds solely on the basis of the lowest cost possible. Penny-wise, perhaps, but almost inevitably pound-foolish.

The wisest way to pick a fund or investment is to examine closely its track record. You're looking for a solid total return over an extended period—five years is a minimum, and I prefer to look at ten years or longer whenever possible.

Each of Cynthia's investments charged only a 1-percent annual fee; in total, they also earned a net 6 percent annually over the twelve years she owned them. Compare that to the funds I showed her—funds that charged about 1.5 percent each year but which returned more than 12-percent net earnings every year on average.

The answer is obvious, and so is the lesson: It matters little what a fund manager is earning from your account as long as you are making *a lot* more. Expenses are important, certainly, but the *return* you actually receive should be your major concern.

Service

Make sure you get what you pay for. In today's world, it's become second nature to always ferret out the best price. That's fine if you're comparing cans of soup. It's not always applicable when you're considering your financial future.

If you're following this book's guidelines and have found a prospective financial advisor you think may walk on water, don't be put off by his fees. Sure, you want to question him closely on why they seem out of line with the marketplace, but if this is counterbalanced by the service you can expect, the premium price may be worthwhile.

Does he schedule regular educational seminars to update his customers? Does an energetic, competent, and efficient staff jump to provide you with the answers when you call or visit? Most important, is he helping to create, grow, and protect wealth for his customers? If so, and if you feel you can afford it, you might want to fly first-class. It's much more comfortable and often worth the additional money.

Accountants

To paraphrase an ancient joke, some of my best friends are accountants. As in all walks of life, there are a wide range of competencies, strengths and . . . well, non-strengths and incompetencies among CPAs and other accounting professionals.

In recent years, some accountants have moved into the wider world of investment advice. A few are good at it, but I urge caution here. These are two different worlds, and each require substantial effort to achieve competency and remain current; it's hard to be both an outstanding accountant and an outstanding financial advisor.

If you need a CPA, look for one who is proactive. By this, I mean you need somebody who will ask penetrating questions of you each year—questions that you would not have even known to ask. Only in that way will he be able to determine the best way to protect your interests, for instance, in helping develop a strategy that minimizes the taxes you pay. You don't want someone whose initiative is limited to filling in the blanks neatly.

Your CPA and your financial advisor must be able to work well together; each has a role to play, and this is an area where two good heads that work in concert can be worth gold to you.

All the above notwithstanding, there are many honest and well-meaning brokers out there. Certainly, not every broker cheats, connives, or manipulates his customers. Many people are, in fact, well served by the people who they trust with their money.

But, as in everything else in life, an ounce of caution can save you a ton of trouble. Trust is the essential component of any broker-client relationship. If you don't get the answers you need, or if those answers don't feel complete or can't be verified, you're well advised to keep looking for help that is both honest and competent. At the very least, now you have a few more questions to ask.

Cynthia learned this lesson the hard way, by missing out on slightly under $50,000 in growth that she could logically have expected to earn in just one area of her portfolio. She also paid needless commissions for trades and investments that left her no better off than when she started. The only upside that came of the sorry mess is that, once alerted, Cynthia took the actions she needed.

Overall I think it must have been a good experience for Cynthia. These days, she supervises her own investment portfolio, but now she knows how to get help when she needs it.

I talked with her a few weeks ago, when she called to set up the review meeting we hold regularly. I look over her statements and records and talk through any problems. I provide advice and answer any questions. And then she pays me on the basis, which she selected, of what she decided she needs.

By the hour.

I couldn't be more proud of her.

Banking on It: A Walk on the Wild Side

Talk about coincidences.

I was sitting at my desk, taking a moment between appointments to make a few final changes to this chapter. I had just penciled in a revision to Cynthia's tale of investment woes, tweaking the part where the brokerage sharks were going into a feeding frenzy of account-churning. At that moment, through the glass wall that separates my private office from the outer business area, I saw a woman come through the front door. She walked straight to the desk where my personal assistant sits. I couldn't hear her through the partition, but she seemed agitated.

As it turned out, the timing of her appearance in my office was uncanny.

Her name was Janet, but I did not recognize her when she came in—not surprising, since I had last seen her almost twenty-two months before, when she had attended one of my annual financial seminars for prospective new clients.

Usually, we will meet with all the people who attend one of my seminars within ninety days of the seminar they attend. When I checked our records, I found that my staff had contacted Janet nine times during that time period, trying to set up an appointment. Her excuses always varied; ultimately, we shrugged and moved on.

But now Janet was here—unexpectedly and apparently with big problems.

As my assistant gave her a cup of hot chocolate and a few forms to fill out, I walked into the waiting room to welcome my visitor. When I invited her into my inner sanctum, Janet grabbed the cup of hot chocolate and snatched up a rather large, bulging bag. Without a word, she dashed into my office.

I followed, studying the forms she had completed.

Janet, fifty-eight, had been widowed almost three years ago. She had two children and three grandchildren (all living out of state), resided in a cozy three-bedroom house (paid off), considered herself ultraconservative (at least in her approach to investments), and had approximately $700,000 in investable assets. And she was furious. I was scarcely seated when Janet was off to the races.

I confess, for the first several moments I could decipher little of what Janet was saying; her words came in a mad rush, she was so outraged. I was tempted to let her vent indefinitely, knowing that it might have been easier to flag down a runaway train. But then I heard her say ". . . now, *now* I find out I have lost more than *twenty-five percent* of my portfolio's value *in just two years!*—" and despite my earlier resolve, I waved my hands in what I hoped was a soothing semaphore until her words slowed and finally sputtered to a stop.

"Something here sounds very, very wrong," I told her. "I hope I can help—but I think I need to ask you a few questions now, and I need you to answer as calmly as possible."

Janet nodded grimly, and I'm sure she really tried. Even so, it took no less than forty-five minutes to fully extract the detailed picture I needed.

The facts: After Janet's husband James died from a sudden stroke, she turned to her local bank for financial counsel. Her reasoning was not unique: After all, if you can't trust your bank, who can you trust?

Like many banks these days, hers had a small department that dealt with investment issues. The in-house broker they assigned to Janet was a young man with a nice smile. He sounded both competent and concerned, and Janet remembered how much better she felt after leaving that appointment.

Then, at first in slow motion but with a steady acceleration, the roof began to collapse on her.

Janet showed me her first statements: They indicated that the broker was busily selling off virtually *all* of her previous holdings. This was pretty dramatic action and a questionable practice in itself. But with the proceeds, the nice young man from the bank was putting Janet into a host of mutual funds and variable annuities—all in the same family of funds. Why?

"He said it would be easier for me to understand," Janet said. She was making a conscious effort to sound calm, but her posture was as tight as a violin string. "Okay—I admit that I never really understood what he was doing. But damn it: I'd tell myself, 'Wasn't *he* the expert?'"

By her next statement, Janet had lost 5 percent of portfolio value. She searched her newspaper, looking for stories about a stock market downturn—an unsuccessful search, since at that time most of the indicators were going *up*.

Janet called her bank broker repeatedly over the next several months, trying to get some answers. No luck there; even when he returned her calls, it seemed like she was left with nothing more than additional questions.

"Finally," Janet admitted, "I just stopped calling."

By now, in my head a familiar melody was playing, loud and insistent. You'd know the tune immediately: *dah-dah-DAH-dah, dah-dah-DAH-dah, dah-dah-DAH-dah* . . .

It was that eerie theme from *The Twilight Zone*.

I handed the manuscript to Janet. "Read this," I said. "You might find this particular chapter very interesting." I sat and watched the expressions on her face as she read about Cynthia's misadventures on the Investment Merry-Go-Round.

After she finished, she sat speechless. Then: "How about my annuities? Did I get stuck there, too?"

I nodded. "You were sold three different annuities, all with six- to nine-year surrender charges."

I saw Janet move from anger to shock and back again; I expected steam from her ears, but I plowed ahead.

"It gets worse," I warned her. "For a fiscal conservative, you're positioned more like a high-risk addict. Your broker actually has about eighty-five percent of your net assets in the stock market. That's the main reason your account nosedived and lost a quarter of its value."

Now I thought that I would have to get the fire extinguisher down off the wall.

"That's not what I told him I wanted!" Janet was almost shouting. "I thought it was the *other* way around!" (There's a very good lesson here: Always ask your broker to tell you exactly what percentage of your money you have in the market and what percentage you have in fixed income. If he tells you not to worry—or even worse, just says "Trust me"—get another broker.)

Now, what was the only real difference between poor Janet and poor Cynthia?

Well, not much. But the major difference is pretty revealing.

Cynthia dealt with a major brokerage house; Janet dealt with a broker at her local bank. A *big* word of caution here: Local banks are not the best places to look for investment advice. Why? Money and ego, pure and simple.

A *good* broker today—one with an established and satisfied client list—can easily earn an income into the high six figures; some annually post seven-figure incomes. Meanwhile, few local bank presidents earn more than $200,000 or so in annual salary.

There aren't a lot of banks that will hire some thirty-two-year-old broker and—through salary and commissions—allow him to make more than the president of the bank. The cream always flows to the top; in hierarchical, tradition-bound institutions like most banks, it *has* to. Conversely, in our open market–type of capitalism, the *best* brokers will always go where they can make the most money—and that is just not at a bank.

We worked hard with Janet trying to undo the damage. But months later, she was only starting to see a portfolio value that each month showed positive returns for her. It will take even longer for her to recover emotionally from her disastrous foray into the shark tank.

When I got to know her better, I asked Janet why she had put us off so many times when we called to set up appointments. She was honest about it.

"I assumed that you would probably be about the same as anybody else," she said. "Besides—it was my *bank*, for crying out loud. I thought I could trust it."

She knows better now. And so do you.

HOW INSURANCE COMPANIES ARE RANKED

Rank Number	A.M. Best	S&P	Moody's	Duff & Phelps	Weiss
1	A++	AAA	Aaa	AAA	A+
2	A+-	AA+	Aa1	AA+	A
3	A	AA	Aa2	AA	A-
4	A-	AA-	Aa3	AA-	B+
5	B++	A+	A1	A+	B
6	B+	A	A2	A	B-
7	B	A-	A3	A-	C+
8	B-	BBB+	Baa1	BBB+	C
9	C++	BBB	Baa2	BBB	C-
10	C+	BBB-	Baa3	BBB-	D+*
11	C	BB+*	Ba1*	BB+*	D

* At this rating and below, the Insurance Forum puts the insurance company on its Watch List.

A Rose by Any Other Name . . .

Over the years, I've examined the portfolios and brokerage account records of literally thousands of prospective clients. In far too many cases, as I explain all the catastrophe that is their financial reality, at some point I've found myself voicing the following inquiry:

"Good heavens! What lunatic were you dealing with when all this happened?"

The usual response: "I trusted him. I mean, his card said he was a senior vice president. A guy that high in the organization—I figured that he must know what he is doing . . ."

Sadly, more often than not they can take that title, add seventy-five cents, and buy a cup of coffee—although not a very good cup of coffee.

Titles at brokerage houses, just as in banks, are frequently given out because it's less expensive to the organization than giving the employee a raise. At any bank or brokerage, if you toss a brick in any direction you will maim a half-dozen "senior vice presidents" and cripple twice as many "directors" or "assistant VPs."

The only title you should be concerned about at a major brokerage house is president or chairman of the board. If you see either of these on the person's business card, you're dealing with a verifiable big shot. Take anything less with a grain of salt; most often, you'll need the whole shaker.

After all, in what universe does it make sense for a twenty-something-year-old to be senior vice president of *anything* other than a college fraternity?

In reality, the bigger the title sounds, the higher you should hoist the caution flags. In brokerage houses, a title is a commodity to be bartered in exchange for sales volume. The more a broker sells to people like you, the bigger the title. When a broker jumps to a new firm, it's standard procedure to ask the new employer to anoint him a vice president. That makes his existing clients believe the move was a promotion, and it makes them more likely to follow the broker to his next firm.

Unfortunately, these titles aren't awarded for what they should reward—to wit, making money for their *clients*. They are passed around for making money for the *firm*. Brokerage houses know down to the last penny how much individual brokers sell daily, weekly, monthly, and annually. They know precisely what investment vehicles and products are being moved by whom; they know every transaction's value to the brokerage's bottom line. But there are no statistics available to base promotions on how well any given broker serves the poor, abused client.

Want to make your big-titled broker squirm? Next time you talk to him, ask exactly what he had to do to "earn" the title. Look interested while he answers and be sure to ask for all the details. In a perfect world, at some point he'd break down and confess: While that's not the world we live in, at least you'll hear some entertaining fiction from your "senior" corporate official.

Chapter 6

"But I'm Too Young to Be a Widow!"

For Nancy, the end of the world came one crisp September morning—incongruously, with the smell of Pop-Tarts in the air and the theme to *Sesame Street* playing in the background.

It was a morning like most: She was in sweater and jeans, and a half hour earlier had waved to her husband John as he left for his morning run—five miles, the same five miles he had run virtually every morning since college. For Nancy, it was a brief time just for herself, with coffee and the newspaper.

Then, she saw the black-and-white police car pull into her driveway and the two officers walk toward her front door.

"My heart stopped—I'm sure of it," Nancy, an attractive woman of thirty-one, remembers. "My first response was to run into the rec room, to make sure both the kids were there. They were eating and watching Big Bird on TV, so I was able to breathe again.

"By then the doorbell was ringing, and I couldn't imagine what was wrong. I thought maybe one of my parents had been in an accident, or had a heart attack. I do recall thinking I'd have to wait for John to return so we could drive to the hospital together."

She shakes her head in memory, and for a moment you can still see the disbelief Nancy must have felt that terrible morning as the police officers asked to enter her home. By their demeanor—somehow too gentle, too polite—she immediately knew it was very, very bad.

"For some reason, I never thought it might have been about John. He went to the health club three or four times a week; he jogged every day. He seemed so strong, so healthy. So . . . so *indestructible*."

So Nancy sat, numb with shock, as one of the officers spoke the awful words: John was dead.

A motorist had found the thirty-three-year-old lying motionless on the side of the road less than two miles from his home, his eyes open and a look of mild surprise on his face. When the weakened artery deep inside his brain had ballooned and burst, he passed from living to dead in less time than it takes to flip a switch.

Nancy walked into my office slightly more than a month later. I was on the phone at the time and idly noticed the tall, athletic-looking young lady talking to my receptionist. I recall thinking it was probably about IRAs or wealth management—the kind of financial planning issues that many people her age often come to discuss with me.

But when I went out to greet her, I noticed The Bag. For Nancy, it was an oversized straw bag, gaily decorated with bright yellow sunflowers—the kind designed for a long day on the beach. I've seen women carrying different versions of The Bag into my office before, and it's always a tipoff that something very bad has entered their world.

I escorted her into my office, trying not to be too obvious as I glanced down into The Bag. Sure enough, it bulged with papers, forms, receipts—definitely, a person who had received bad news.

How bad, I immediately discovered. Nancy blinked once or twice, and then her words poured out in a torrent: "My husband is dead, I have two kids, no job, the mortgage is due, the lease payment on my car is overdue. *And I don't have any money!*"

I brought out the box of tissues and handed several to Nancy. Then I put the box on the desk between us—a good idea, as it turned out, since as she told her story, I needed more than a few for myself.

Nancy rummaged through The Bag for a moment, then handed me what she found. It was a photo, apparently taken a month or two earlier at an end-of-summer picnic. There was Nancy, seated between two children—John Jr., six, and Lisa, three—alongside a handsome man, their deceased father, John.

"This is—*was*—my family," she said. "It's the last picture I'll ever have of all of us together."

We both kept it together, but just barely.

I've heard some financial advisors talk about how they have to maintain a professional reserve, no matter what; I've never been able to, not completely. Unless you're a monster, you can't hear a story like Nancy's and stay dry-eyed.

Of course, Nancy didn't really need my sympathy. She had already gotten a lot of that from the other people in her life, particularly in the days and even weeks after the funeral. At first, there were frequent calls from her friends; some even dropped by every day or so to make sure she was holding up. They would bring over lunch, help with the kids, linger over coffee with the new widow. But as time went by, the calls and visits came less frequently. All of a sudden, it dawned on Nancy that the people that she used to see all the time—when, like them, she was part of a couple—now just . . . stayed away.

Nancy realized that she was on her own, and it terrified her.

Nancy and John had been classic " 'tweeners," straddling the line between Generation Xer and Yuppie. They had spent money freely, even after the birth of their children. Life was good and times were golden; tomorrow always looked even brighter. Unfortunately, like most couples their age, there really was not much in the way of savings, equity, or investing. Nancy was a homemaker. John had worked himself up to the manager of a large independent sporting goods store. The prospects for advancement were good, but even with bonuses and commissions, John had earned about $68,000 the year before. This sounds like a lot, and it can be—but not if you have two growing kids, a big mortgage, and are incurring all the other expenses of a youthful, optimistic life.

Unfortunately for Nancy, at least in hindsight, the

money had been enough to allow the family to purchase a new $186,000 home two years before with a minimal down payment. Nice house, but bad news: In two years of payments, they had built virtually no equity yet. And there was more bad news: When you buy a new-construction home, there is almost always a builder's markup of at least 20 percent. In the first three years or so, you're in the hole. It's almost impossible to resell for what you paid, particularly when you factor in real estate commissions.

For Nancy, bad became even worse: To get the down payment of about $30,000 on the house, Nancy and John had accepted the lion's share in the form of an unreported loan from Nancy's father. (In actual fact, they broke the law to do this. Banks always ask whether you borrowed money to get your down payment; it's on the mortgage's disclosure form.) Legal loan or not, unless Nancy wanted to stiff her father, it was a debt that needed to be repaid. And Nancy's father was not a rich man.

"Did John have life insurance?" I asked. Especially for younger couples, this is often the bulk of the deceased estate.

At that point, Nancy just began to cry. Before she spoke, I had guessed what she was going to say. I had heard it far too many times before.

"John had a $100,000 whole-life policy," Nancy said. "His company didn't offer life insurance, so he bought it through a college friend."

I winced. Some friend.

Whole-life policies are the wrong type of insurance for most people, but especially for most younger people. They are designed *first* as a long-term savings plan and only *secondarily* as a life insurance plan. Insurance should be bought to cover risk, not to serve as an investment. Insurance agents know this, but they sell "friends" on whole-life plans nevertheless. Why? Quite simply, greed. It is not uncommon for a life insurance agent to earn *ten times* the commission on a whole-life policy than he would on a term plan that provides the same death-benefit payout. Put another way, depending on your age, it's possible to buy up to six times as much in term coverage as the same premium would purchase in whole-life insurance. Translated, for a young adult, that can mean about $500,000 worth of term insurance for perhaps $500 per year—comparatively, a bargain.

But with whole-life, the result is a higher cost for less insurance, as Nancy discovered. After she paid all the bills and funeral costs, that $100,000 payout had already shrunk significantly. Left in Nancy's checking account was approximately $91,000—better than nothing, but far less than the debt load she carried and woefully inadequate for a widow with two young children.

By now, I had used almost as much tissue as had Nancy. How was I going to help this woman? Remember our Step 1? The very first thing I told Nancy to do was to take a deep breath. Next, we defined the circumstances she faced, clearly and concisely. We made a written list that said:

- Nancy is a thirty-one-year-old widow with two young children.
- She has no job, few marketable skills, and less than a year of college education.
- She has payments on the $186,000 house, a $30,000 loan from her father to repay; in total, these debts exceed the market value of the property.

- She has no insurance (life or health coverage) on herself or her children; if the worst happened to her, she also had no current will or living trust to protect them.
- She has a $479 a month lease payment against the car, which still has thirty-four months to go on the payment.
- She owes about $2,200 in various credit card balances.
- And her only cash asset is $91,000 in the bank—and if she tried to live on that principal, even under the most optimistic circumstances, she would be broke within two to three years.

This list is essential. It allows a person to see that what she faces may be daunting, but it is also quantifiable. Rather than an overwhelming barrage of unsolvable catastrophes, she can see it is a point-by-point *problem* that can be solved by addressing each issue on the list.

"What I'm going to ask you to do now may sound hard," I told her. "But I want you to go home and read this list. Not once, but several times. Read it until you can recite it. And then I want you to do one more thing." I took the list from her hand, wrote for a minute, and pushed it across the desk to Nancy. "We've just created a category called 'New Goals.' Under New Goals, there are four headings: immediate goals, short-term goals, intermediate-term goals, and long-term goals. When you come back, I want to talk about what you've listed there."

"Is that all?" she asked, and I'm sure she was wondering if she had made a mistake coming to see me.

"Not quite," I said. "When you return, don't come alone. Who do you feel closest to in the world, aside from your children?"

"My dad," she said, not surprisingly. "And my mother. They live nearby, in town."

"We'll meet again in two weeks; ask them to come with you. We're going to work together to help you fix all this."

Nancy arrived early for our next meeting; the first thing I noticed was that she was not carrying The Bag. That's usually a good sign; it was for Nancy, as was the fact that she no longer looked like a person who was carrying the weight of the world on her shoulders. As I greeted her near our reception desk, the door opened and I could see two of the reasons why. Her parents were with her today.

It was obvious that her father Robert was a person that loved to laugh. He had that kind of face—it was split by a grin both wide and infectious—and he walked with a relaxed grace that spoke volumes. With him was Nancy's mother, Betty, who might have stepped right from a Norman Rockwell painting that featured Christmas cookies and the grandkids gathered around. Together, they seemed to exude an aura of homey warmth that comforted Nancy.

But it was also obvious that Nancy related strongly to her father as an individual. He was the man who had taught her to ride her first bike and had cheered her on in swim meets, gymnastic competitions, and soccer games. He had taught her how to throw a softball; he had held the camera proudly as she had accepted her diploma. He was, in short, her anchor. And it showed.

"I hear you're going to help my little girl," Robert said, his oversized hand easily encompassing mine.

"I'm willing to try," I said. "That is, if *you* are."

For just an instant, I saw Robert and Betty stiffen. I already knew why.

Robert and Betty were not rich, certainly not by today's standards. As we talked, I learned a few relevant details: They had some money in CDs, and a few stock investments they had made over the years. All told, as Robert neared his retirement, their total liquid net worth was perhaps $260,000—adequate, especially since their home was paid off. But the lion's share of their retirement income would come from Robert's pension, which they planned to draw on when he stopped working in perhaps a year's time.

"But if I need to—if it would help Nancy—I can put off retirement for another year or two," Robert said. "I know she's going to need some help, even if she goes out and gets herself a job now." He reached over and patted his daughter's hand.

Why was all this important?

If Nancy was to succeed at turning her life around, Robert and Betty would have to make a major commitment, financial as well as emotional. That was underscored by a simple, albeit personally devastating, fact: Nancy's house would have to be sold. There just was not enough money to keep it.

"So she either has to find another place of her own," I said, "or there are three new people living with Grandma and Grandpa."

I watched the three of them process that information. Nancy's eyes were hooded, hiding what could only have been the shame she felt. Robert looked as if he were doing sums in his head, but not like a man faced with anything more than a problem to be solved. Betty seemed thrilled at the idea—the prospect of her daughter returning home, especially with the grandchildren in tow seemed to her anything but daunting.

"We can swing it," Robert said, finally. "But it doesn't seem to solve all Nancy's problems."

"It doesn't," I agreed. "It's not a permanent solution in any way. But it gives Nancy the breathing room she needs to solve them herself. Nancy, could I see your list of New Goals now?"

She passed me the paper. At the top, in large letters she had underscored several times, it said, "Survive the next twelve months."

Good; we were on the same wavelength, more or less.

What was in the best interest of Nancy, of her parents, of her children to do next?

Essentially, there were two basic options. First, Nancy could focus on the short term; she could look for a job. I'm in favor of people working, but in Nancy's case there were some basic drawbacks. She had no college degree and few, if any, marketable skills. That meant little chance of a job that would provide more than starvation wages, and that even without factoring in the cost of child care while she was working. It could also doom her to a lifetime of dependency on her parents' generosity or force her to remarry simply for financial security.

Option Two took the longer view: Should Nancy be looking at possibly going back to school? Earning a degree and being trained in something she enjoyed would entail definite immediate sacrifices. But over the long haul, did it give her the possibility of a far better life? Without a doubt.

But it was important for Robert and Betty to understand what all this would mean to them. First, at least in the next few years, as a student Nancy would be exceptionally dependent on them for financial support; so would her children. Early retirement would no longer be an option for Robert. Nor would Robert and Betty enjoy the same life they had been living as empty-nesters. Privacy, child-free serenity, and many of the freedoms associated with their maturity and age would be gone. And because Robert would be the male authority figure in the house, he would be, in effect, "adopting" his own grandchildren, serving as the *de facto* father figure.

Nancy: Single working mom, or dependent college student/daughter? Which was the better course of action, for *all* concerned?

The more we talked, the more everybody seemed to like the second option. Especially Robert; instead of rushing out to get a job, if Nancy earned a college degree, she'd be significantly better off in the long term . . . and everybody could look down the road where she could achieve financial independence again. On our "to do" list, I wrote a note to investigate available government low-interest loans and grants to help finance Nancy's education.

But that did not mean Nancy would not work. She would have to, for a very important reason that had nothing to do with a paycheck. Not by coincidence, this focused on the second "New Goals" item Nancy had listed: "Protect my kids' future."

"I hated to put that second," she said.

I nodded. "Not to worry," I said. "It's all linked together. I'll show you what I mean."

With two small children, Nancy needed to have good health insurance. She was going to collect some money from John's Social Security benefits, but scarcely enough to pay for the ever-rising cost of good medical coverage. I recommended that Nancy should look for part-time employment, concentrating less on the salary than on the benefits offered. Even in a recession, jobs remain unfilled at large supermarket chains, bookstores, law firms, accounting services, and even some large corporations. These operations often look for good people willing to work fifteen or so hours a week—and many of them provide the same level of health insurance benefits to part-time workers as they do to their full-time staff.

Speaking of insurance, what about life insurance? This was a more difficult problem: Few companies provide more than a nominal coverage, if that. Here, Nancy was going to have to dig into her own funds. Her kids needed the security of a large-coverage policy.

The good news: Because of her good health and her relatively young age, Nancy could buy $500,000 of term life insurance for a few hundred dollars a year. On our "to do" list, I penciled in a note to that effect.

It was now that I raised, as delicately as possible, the logical next question: What would happen to her children if the worst happened to Nancy? She had no plan in place.

My recommendation: set up a living trust. In her living trust document, she would provide a plan for the care and guidance of her children in the event of her death. This is, of course, a weighty consideration. Her parents were the logical candidates, but they were in their mid-sixties now; could they handle such a task? Should they?

So we made it another "to do" item: Make a list of at least three sets of potential guardians for the kids. Why three sets? To ensure there would be someone of Nancy's choosing available. Otherwise, the courts would decide what would happen to her children.

We turned to the next item on Nancy's New Goals list: "Get out of debt this year."

Again, an excellent goal for a new widow—very specific, and one we could begin to work on immediately, if only by selling that white elephant of a house. Certainly, there were complications in this. Because Nancy and John had purchased a new house, it would take several years to build up even a modest equity. It is a cruel equation: John and Nancy paid $186,000, the market price for new construction; in two years of mortgage payments, they had paid almost $30,000—but most of that was interest. They had paid only about $2,000 against the mortgage balance. To break even on the sale, Nancy would have to ask for about $200,000. (Remember: She would pay at least 6-percent commission to a broker, and probably more.)

But comparable new housing was still priced at about $190,000. Ouch.

Clearly, getting Nancy's money out of her house was not going to be easy. But there were a few tricks we could try. For instance, I suggested to Nancy that she try to sell the house by owner, not through a real estate broker. That would allow her to lower the price by approximately $12,000, to about $178,000—lower than some of the other new houses in the neighborhood. And if the house did not sell in the first month, Nancy could still list it with a broker. Either way, Nancy was going to incur a loss on the sale, because there was Robert's loan of $30,000 to be repaid. But the sooner we freed her from her mortgage and property tax debt load, the better.

Next, we turned to her car expense. The car Nancy and John had leased still had thirty-four months to run, at $439 per month. Far too much for her new circumstances. So our options were either to sell the car (and pay the difference between the sale price and the residual owed), get out of the lease agreement, or find a third party with acceptable credit to take over the lease.

I instructed Nancy to contact the leasing company—in this case it was General Motors—and to ask them if they would cancel the lease. Sometimes leasing companies will, particularly in circumstances like those Nancy faced.

Robert looked at Betty, and raised a second possibility. "Heck, we need a new car anyway," he said. "And I've always liked yours, baby." He turned to Nancy. "If GM won't come through, we will."

It was a major relief. Either way, Nancy would now be in a position to buy a reliable secondhand car. It wouldn't be fancy, and it definitely would be cheap—$10,000 to $12,000, tops. It would also be all Nancy needed, and what she could afford to spend. Actually, even less: I advised her to put down 50 percent of the money and take a loan out for the other 50 percent. Why? It would help build up her credit rating in her own name.

And knowing what you can afford is critical. That's why Nancy, *like everybody else,* needed to draw up a written budget. This is not to be taken lightly or without the proper tools. One of the tools I provided Nancy, a sample budget form, is printed in this chapter (see pages 111–13).

As you can see, the form provides a sample budget that divides entries into three separate categories: annual income, fixed expenses, and nonfixed expenses.

Let's look at each, in turn.

Annual income is every dollar you take in: salary, wages, tips, interest from CDs or savings, commissions, any Social Security benefits you collect, dividends from stock holdings—the whole enchilada. If you can reasonably expect a bonus, a lot of people want to add it in, too, but usually it's best not to. Too many times, I've heard people say, "I don't know what happened. I thought I was certain to get that bonus." Same thing with gifts. In this category, you want to list *only* the money you can count on.

Too strict for you? Okay, I'll give you a break here: If you are 95 percent sure that money is coming in, go ahead and put it down. But that's as venturesome as I'll let you get.

Under *fixed expenses* generally what you list are those expenses that you know are there, come hell or high water. Expenses in this category are the ones that are impossible to avoid and usually really hard to reduce. It is just like the name implies: They are fixed.

Examples? At the top of your list, there is Uncle Sam, and all his nieces and nephews at the state and local levels. Then there is housing; even when you own your own mortgage-free property, there are still fixed expenses such as insurance, utilities, general maintenance, telephone, cable TV, and property taxes.

If you notice, in this category I have also included a replacement fund. Why? Quite simply, because sooner or later you will need to have one. Every major business does, and your needs are just as important as theirs. This is money you put aside each year to replace big-ticket items—the furnace, air conditioner, or roof, for instance. An air conditioner can cost $3,000 to replace; if you put $250 away every year, fifteen years down the road you can pay for that new air conditioner (including a margin for inflation) without going into debt. The same principle works for cars, which can allow you to be one of those very rare people who live without a monthly car payment.

Which brings us to other fixed expenses—specifically, transportation-related costs like gas, insurance, routine maintenance. Then there are tollway fees, parking, all the other costs associated with owning a car.

Remember insurance? You need life insurance, health insurance, even disability insurance. People in their forties are eight times more likely to become disabled than to die outright. The drawback: Disability insurance is very expensive.

Getting older? How about nursing-care insurance? More and more people, staggered at the costs they see their parents are incurring, are opting to buy nursing home care when they reach their early fifties. One or two generations down the road, people will be buying nursing home care as commonly as they buy homeowners insurance.

If you are like Nancy, you have children; add the expenses associated with raising kids. Child care, clothes, even birthday gifts—figure it all in.

Don't stop here. As you fill in the budget form, you'll think of more.

The third category we look at is called, logically enough, *nonfixed expenses*. There are three different categories listed: personal, entertainment, and financial. These are expenses you can take or leave; you have a great amount of control over them.

Do you dine out? You can choose to eat at home, instead. Vacations? Ditto. Clothes? If you are a slave to fashion, it is going to cost you here. Cosmetics, laundry, dry cleaning, charities, cell phone, gifts, anniversaries—all come under the nonfixed category.

How about your financial decisions? Do you contribute to a 401(k), an IRA, a Roth Account, or a retirement savings plan? How about your children's education fund, your own student loans, personal bank loans outstanding? And don't forget your personal emergency fund. You need enough money to fund you for three to six months in a crunch, and you have to build this fund with a monthly set-aside in savings.

With all this information in hand, you do just what Nancy had to do: From your total annual income, subtract all your fixed expenses and all your nonfixed expenses. Bingo. What is left is disposable income (if it's a positive number) or the deficit you will be facing at the end of the year.

And I'll give you the same advice I give my clients, and that I gave Nancy. Make sure your budget leaves a little room to have a little bit of fun. Otherwise, it's just like a too-strict diet: You won't stay on it.

Back to Nancy's list. The final item on it read: "Prepare myself for the rest of my life." Again, not a minor goal; again, one we could begin to work on immediately.

The $91,000 Nancy had in her account from John's insurance was the key, of course. After she bought a car, and earmarked about $15,000 for an emergency fund, she was going to have perhaps $60,000 with which to work. Rather than just dropping it into a CD, I urged her to think slightly more aggressively.

What I recommended was a carefully selected host of mutual funds called "hybrid funds." These funds simply maintain approximately 60 percent of their assets in stock investments and 40 percent in the bond market. They're also known as "balanced funds," and many of them have a record of providing good returns over the long haul. Even better, they incur less risk than most garden-variety stock mutual funds.

Here's why: In any 60/40 program (60 percent of your money in stock, 40 percent in bonds) the bonds are intended as the conservative, "safe" component. When the stock market stumbles, presumably the bonds will buffer your overall portfolio value. The same is true on the flip side: When the market is screaming along, the bonds tend to hold you back. But with a hybrid fund, you take the middle road. You may never hit a home run, but you won't strike out either. At this time in her life, that's a good strategy for Nancy.

We picked out a number of hybrid funds that carried a five-star rating by Morningstar; that is, funds that were in the top 10 percent of their kind. Generally, these funds tend to invest in major blue-chip companies, mixed with a few carefully selected growth stocks. By following this strategy, at least until Nancy had her feet underneath her sometime in the future, we could expect both an acceptable risk and a decent rate of growth for her capital.

Then I turned on my most disarming smile.

"You most likely aren't thinking about this now," I said to Nancy, "but you will, because it's natural. Some-day, you're going to consider getting married again. You need to think about that—maybe not today, but in the near future."

(To help her if and when that time came, I told Nancy a story about a client of mine named Jenny. I've repeated Jenny's story in the following chapter.)

There is much to be learned from Nancy's case, but it all comes down to a single question, whether you are eigh-teen or eighty. Ask yourself this: Would you be prepared if your spouse walked out the door one morning and never re-turned?

By the time we were done that day, Nancy had a much better idea of what to do. So did her parents. All of us un-derstood it would not be easy, but now Nancy had her plan and the will to stick to it.

Two weeks later, Nancy called. She sounded good—excited, and even with a touch of joy in her tone. The plan for her was already working, she said. The house was on the market, and the kids were excited about moving in with their grandparents. Even more thrilling, Nancy announced that she was going to be a teacher—that is, after she gradu-ated from the local college that had accepted her as an edu-cation major.

Nancy had even made progress on the other areas of her new plan. She was working part-time at a retail chain bookstore not far from her college campus. While the pay was low, the benefits provided the health coverage for her and her children. She even had talked to the student legal aid department, which assigned a final-year law student to help her set up the living trust.

"For free," Nancy said, and I smiled at the newfound confidence in her voice.

Nancy was on her way.

SAMPLE BUDGET

	Amount/Annually	Amount/Monthly
ANNUAL INCOME		
Salary/Wages/Tips	$	$
Commissions	$	$
Bonuses (95% chance)	$	$
Interest Income (CDs, Savings Act., etc.)	$	$
Social Security	$	$
Gifts (95% sure of)	$	$
Pensions	$	$
Rents/Royalties	$	$
Tax Refunds/Rebates	$	$
Extra Income	$	$
Income Totals	$	$
FIXED EXPENSES		
Taxes		
Federal Taxes	$	$
State Taxes	$	$
Local Taxes	$	$
FICA Taxes	$	$
Other Taxes	$	$
Taxes Totals	$	$
Housing		
Mortgage/Rent	$	$
Insurance	$	$
Utilities	$	$
Maintenance (clean carpets, fix roof, etc.)	$	$
Condo Association Fees	$	$
Telephone	$	$
Cable TV	$	$
Cable Modem	$	$
Buy/Replace Furniture Fund	$	$
Parking	$	$
Replacement Fund (money put aside yearly to replace large items—furnace, AC, roof, etc.)	$	$
Others	$	$
Housing Totals	$	$

	Amount/Annually	Amount/Monthly
Transportation		
Gas	$	$
Insurance	$	$
Maintenance	$	$
Public Transportation (bus, cab, etc.)	$	$
Tolls	$	$
License/Registration/Plates	$	$
Car/Lease Payment	$	$
Replacement Fund (money put aside every year to purchase new automobile)	$	$
Others	$	$
Transportation Totals	$	$
Insurance		
Life Insurance	$	$
Health Insurance	$	$
Disability Insurance	$	$
Nursing Home Insurance	$	$
Others	$	$
Insurance Totals	$	$
Children		
Babysitters	$	$
Childcare	$	$
Clothes	$	$
Alimony	$	$
Child Support	$	$
Toys	$	$
Prescriptions/Doctors/Dentists	$	$
Gifts	$	$
Others	$	$
Children Totals	$	$
Fixed Expenses Totals		
Taxes Total	$	$
Housing Total	$	$
Transportation Total	$	$
Insurance Total	$	$
Children Total	$	$
Total All Fixed Expenses	$	$
NON-FIXED EXPENSES		
Personal		
Groceries	$	$
Dining Out	$	$
Lunches (work related)	$	$
Clothes	$	$
Shoes	$	$
Haircuts	$	$
Cosmetics	$	$
Laundry/Dry Cleaning	$	$
Health Club Memberships	$	$

	Amount/Annually	Amount/Monthly
Cell phones	$	$
Toiletries	$	$
Charities	$	$
Gifts/Birthdays/Anniversaries	$	$
Others	$	$
Personal Totals	$	$
Entertainment		
Vacations	$	$
Movies/Theater/Plays/Concerts	$	$
Subscriptions/Books/Newspapers	$	$
Dating	$	$
Hobbies	$	$
Pets	$	$
Lessons	$	$
Computers	$	$
Others	$	$
Entertainment Totals	$	$
Financial		
Retirement Plan/Work/401K	$	$
IRA/Roth IRA	$	$
Monthly Savings/Mutual Funds/Stock	$	$
Children's Education Fund	$	$
Emergency Fund	$	$
Credit Card Bills	$	$
New House Fund	$	$
Savings Account	$	$
Student Loans	$	$
Personal Bank Loans	$	$
Tuition	$	$
Others	$	$
Financial Totals	$	$
Non-Fixed Expenses Totals		
Personal Totals	$	$
Entertainment Totals	$	$
Financial Totals	$	$
Total All Non-Fixed Expenses	$	$

	ANNUAL INCOME	$
minus	**ANNUAL FIXED EXPENSES**	$
minus	**ANNUAL NON-FIXED EXPENSES**	$
equals	**TOTAL SURPLUS OR DEFICIT**	$

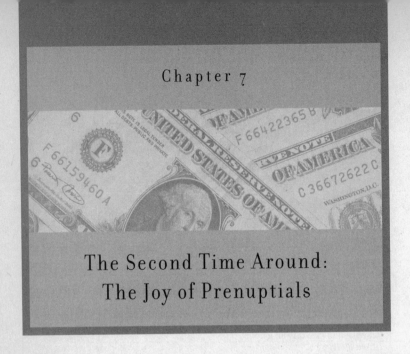

Chapter 7

The Second Time Around: The Joy of Prenuptials

As I hung up the telephone with Nancy, I couldn't help thinking of one hurdle she was still going to have to confront somewhere down the line: At some point, a woman of her age would likely be faced with the prospect of remarriage.

And that always makes me think about Jenny.

Jenny was a client several years ago. She did not end up as one of my success stories, but I think what happened to her is important for many of you reading this book.

Jenny was a wonderful lady. At the time, she was in her early fifties, very attractive, outgoing, vibrant. You probably know what I mean: Jenny was the kind of person who can walk in the room and make it feel as if the sun has come out. She had lost her husband to cancer after a long agonizing fight. Steve had always told her he would make it to her fiftieth-birthday party, and he did—by two days. I never had the pleasure of meeting Steve, but by all the stories Jenny told, he seemed to have been her true soul mate.

Another widow client whom I had helped for years attended Steve's funeral and referred Jenny to me. For the first four years of our advisor-client relationship, things couldn't have been better. Her portfolio value rose steadily, to about $725,000; from the interest, she was drawing a monthly check that covered all her bills. Her four-bedroom house was paid off, she had just purchased a new car. By most measures, she was financially set for the rest of her life.

At the same time, she had grown into her new situation. Jenny asked questions when she didn't understand, and I could see her confidence swell. I could have used her as a perfect example of someone who was doing absolutely everything right to get her life back on track. Jenny even had the enviable pleasure of three married daughters and five grandchildren living nearby, so visits were only minutes away.

So when did the walls start to come crashing down? I remember it, to the day.

Jenny was in my office for one of our semiannual reviews, but I could tell there was definitely something on her mind—and it wasn't money.

"Okay, Jenny—time to 'fess up." I smiled. "Do you want to talk about it?"

She did. "I've met a man," she said, and the floodgates opened.

Her newfound friend was named Jack, and Jenny was obviously smitten. Jenny spoke and spoke of Jack's many virtues, elaborating here and there, occasionally blushing and once even stammering. From her account, Jack seemed a helluva catch—faster than a speeding bullet, able to leap tall buildings with a single bound, more powerful than a locomotive.

And then she dropped the bombshell: "Jack asked me to marry him and I said . . . *yes!*"

This was serious. Jenny was in love, or at the very least she thought she was. As both friend and financial counselor, I needed to know more.

Jack was sixty-one, had been married twice before, and was currently out of work (his company, he had told Jenny, was downsizing). Jack lived in an apartment not far from Jenny's church, which is where the two of them had met.

I wanted to be happy for Jenny, and on some level I was. But there was something troubling about her story that I could not quite verbalize. Statistically, for people aged fifty or younger who divorce or lose their spouse, slightly under 75 percent will remarry. Sadly, around a quarter of those remarriages end in divorce within five years. Jenny was close enough in age that she almost fit into this demographic; more relevant, her vivacious personality made her seem younger than her years. Who wouldn't like to be around her? Plus, she had a measure of wealth—when you considered all her property, a net worth approaching the seven-figure range.

"I'll bet your kids have an opinion about all this," I said, grinning.

Jenny rolled her eyes, but she was smiling when she spoke. "Oh, yes," she said, and made her voice a singsong. " 'Are you *positive* you're ready, Mother?' 'He's not like Daddy, Mom.' You know, David; that sort of thing." She shrugged, trying to make light of it. "I'm sure they just want me to be happy. They just need to get to know Jack better."

I nodded. But I knew Jenny's daughters. They were bright and levelheaded, much like their mother. If something about Jack bothered them, I was not ready to dismiss their concerns out of hand.

Let me translate. What Jenny's daughters were really asking her was "What happens if this leech takes you for everything you own?"

"Well, it looks like a good time to start planning things," I said. "You'll want to protect your own financial security and your daughters' inheritance, of course. We should start thinking about your prenup."

Jenny looked startled.

"Do you think that's necessary?" she asked.

I nodded, deadly serious, and started in on a fast primer course for Jenny to consider. I could tell that Jenny *heard* every word I said but that she wasn't *listening*. She could talk to me about the dates to the movies, how Jack could cook a romantic meal, the night at the opera—all the fun of courtship. But when I asked her if she had discussed their personal finances with Jack, she looked at me as if I were a leper.

Basically, as unromantic as it might sound, a prenuptial agreement lets both parties determine in advance the consequences if a marriage fails. As with all preventive medicine, the taste is not always sugar-sweet. But an ounce of prevention can prevent a pound of often incurable misery.

But the more I talked, the more Jenny withdrew. In her eyes, I had changed. I was no longer her trusted financial advisor and confidant, but instead had metamorphosed into a fin-faced monster from some low-budget '60s sci-fi flick.

I tried anyway.

"If Jack really loves you, cares about you and your family, and wants to spend the rest of his life with you—" I said, and raised my palms. "C'mon, Jenny. He can't object to discussing the subject, at the very least. For the sake of your daughters and their kids—heck, even for the sake of your own financial welfare—you have to explore this with Jack."

She nodded, and I told myself that was a good sign.

I outlined what a prenuptial agreement did: If the marriage did not work out, our goal was for Jenny to exit the marriage with the same assets she had at the start. If she died during the marriage, I explained that most states will give at least one-third of an estate to the surviving spouse, no matter what your will says (check your state's rules for full details); if this was not satisfactory to her, she needed to do something before the marriage.

Jenny pulled out her legal pad and started to take some notes. Here's what I told her:

1.   Both parties should have their own lawyer to advise them on the merits of the legal agreement.

2.   Both parties must give complete disclosure about what assets they have before the marriage. If either party tries to withhold assets, a judge could later void the whole contract or claim fraud.

3.   Nothing can be oral! Everything *must* be in writing and the final agreement signed by both parties. Some states will require your signatures to be notarized.

4. If you decide to go ahead with a prenuptial agreement, have the lawyers videotape the signing. This way, no one can claim they were coerced.

5. Don't make the agreement too lopsided for one side or another. A judge may look very unfavorably on this at a later date.

6. Have the document signed well before the wedding date. Courts hate to see a prenuptial signed on the Friday before the Saturday wedding. It makes it look like a last-minute decision that neither party had time to fully contemplate.

And then I gave Jenny some questions that desperately needed answers before any decision should be made:

1. How will the income that both parties receive be handled every year?

2. Will they file separate or joint tax returns?

3. How will the monthly expenses be paid? Equally or on some percentage basis?

4. How will credit cards be handled? Will they be in single or joint name?

5. Is there a personal business involved? What will happen to it should there be a divorce?

6. Unlikely in this case, but if one spouse helps another through school, how will that spouse be compensated if a divorce occurs?

7. Whose house will they live in? How will the other spouse be compensated for using their home?

8. If either spouse inherits anything during the marriage, how will it be treated?

9.   If they decide to purchase any new property while married, how will it be titled and how will it be paid for?

10.   How will each spouse's funds be distributed in case either party dies during the marriage?

11.   Will their house be sold if either party dies, or will the surviving spouse be able to live there until he or she dies or remarries?

12.   Will either party pay alimony or support, in case of divorce or separation?

13.   Will any children be living with you at any time? If so, who pays their expenses and handles their care?

14.   How will family holidays be spent? (Don't laugh. This one can rank right up there with money itself for causing problems.)

"Enough, enough already. I get the picture."

I could see that this was probably information overload for Jenny, but I hoped I had accomplished my goal. At the very least, Jenny now had enough information to see the value of a prenuptial contract

Jenny stood, hugged me, and thanked me for all my help and support. I patted her shoulder, relieved; Jenny was back up and on the right course again. Everything was right in the world.

How wrong I was. Jenny called three days later. She needed to see me—*right away!*—and she wanted to bring Jack along. I shuffled my schedule and booked them for the next morning.

Uh-oh. When they came through the front door, Jack was leading the way. He moved as if he owned the place; Jenny followed meekly. While he waited, Jack never sat; instead, he paced like a petulant tomcat and I knew there was a storm brewing.

I walked into the reception area to greet them and invited them to have a cup of coffee. Jack glared at me. "We won't be here that long," he said in a tight voice.

Jack weighed about one hundred eighty pounds and carried it well on his six-feet-two frame; he had big hands and a deep, throaty manner of speech. He was good-looking for a man of his age, and I could see why Jenny was drawn to him.

"I understand that you advised Jenny to get a prenuptial agreement drawn up before we get married."

"That's right."

"That's not going to happen," he said. "We talked it over and decided that what's mine is hers and what's hers is mine, period."

"That's not the best way to—"

He waved me off. "In addition, we decided we don't like the way you've been handling Jenny's money. We're going to add her money to mine. My broker can handle it all, and he'll do a better job."

I looked at Jenny. "You agree to all this?"

Tears had started to well up in her eyes, and I knew this was not of her doing. But Jenny just nodded "Yes. That's what we decided."

I knew it was useless, but I spent the next few minutes trying to convince Jenny that she was making a mistake. As Jenny shook her head at each of my suggestions, Jack just glared at me.

Finally he stood. "Come on, Jenny," he said, and Jenny rose, too.

"Jenny," I said. "Why won't you let me help you?"

"I have to trust Jack," she said, and left.

I didn't hear from Jenny after that, not for almost two years. In an odd way, I was relieved. Somehow, I had equated "no news" with "good news." I even convinced my-self that I had misjudged Jack.

So when Jenny called and asked to see me, I hoped it was as two good friends who hadn't seen each other in a very long time. But the Jenny who came into my office wasn't the same woman I had come to know. She had aged beyond her years; her attitude was that of a person accus-tomed to the rain cloud that dogged her every step. We passed a couple of halfhearted pleasantries, but I knew that this was not a social call.

As it had almost twenty-four months before, the story poured from Jenny in a rush. I sat and listened to it all: how it had been so good at the start, when Jack moved from his apartment into Jenny's house; how Jack bought a new car and a whole new wardrobe for himself. But then the argu-ments began. First, over the kids, then, inevitably, over the money.

"I never really looked at our financial statements," Jenny admitted. "Jack insisted on handling it all. Then one day his broker called looking for Jack. I asked him for the total value of our account—" She stopped, unable to con-tinue for a moment.

Then Jenny shook herself. "He said we had 'about' $470,000. I couldn't believe it, David. I had $725,000; Jack put in his own money, too. How could the portfolio be so badly depleted?"

Her mouth formed a tight line. "Well, I found out, all

right. The account started with $725,000 of my money—
and only $11,000 from Jack, all he had. We had lost more
than $90,000 on bad stock trades and the rest was just . . .
gone."

When she confronted Jack, the downward spiral accel-
erated. He told Jenny to stay out of his business.

Then the physical abuse started.

"David, he was living in *my* house," she said. "I
couldn't get him to leave. At last, *I* had to go."

"Jenny, I'm so sorry."

"The divorce was final early last month," she said. "It's
taken me this long to work up enough courage to come in
here. I need your help, David. My life is in pieces, and I
don't know how to put them back together again."

And so we started. It was anything but easy: Jenny had
a lot of pieces scattered around the financial landscape. Her
once-proud portfolio, which had taken a lifetime for her
and her late husband to accumulate, was devastated. After
lawyers' fees and as a lump-sum payoff to Jack to end the
marriage quickly, it had been looted by almost half. Barely
$400,000 remained, and she was lucky to have that much
left. Only a sympathetic judge—an experienced jurist who
had seen through Jack's motives—had allowed Jenny to
walk away with what remained of her money, with her old
house, and with what little personal dignity she had left.

Since then, we've started to repair some of the financial
damage. But it still won't be easy for Jenny. In our last review, I warned her that she may have to sell her house and
find a smaller place to live. Without doubt, she will have to
go back to work—if only for a few years, so her investments
can be left alone to grow.

There is good news, too. Jenny is free of Jack now and wiser for the experience. And she's living testimony to the value of a prenuptial agreement—drawn up, signed, and sealed before the wedding.

But there's bad news too; of course, it involves Jack. You see, he's still out there, looking for wife number four.

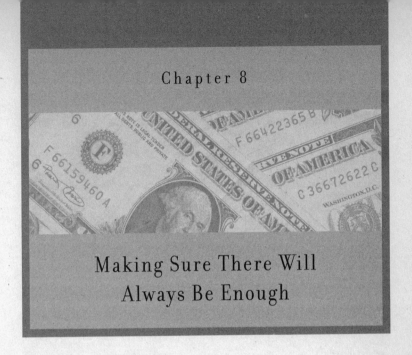

Chapter 8

Making Sure There Will Always Be Enough

Coming home from a financial planning seminar, I was waiting for my luggage to come down the express chute at Chicago's O'Hare airport one summer night. While I waited, the usual thoughts were going through my head. You know the ones, the same ones everybody has. Did *all* my luggage make it back? What am I going to do if my ride home doesn't show up? Boy, I bet the mail at the office is a mile high waiting for me. And did I remember to pay all the bills before I left?

But this time something else stuck in my mind. Rather, *somebody* else, a lady I had just met on the airplane.

Usually I hate to even think about who I may end up sitting next to on a long flight. Every time I set out for an airport my mind replays the old John Candy and Steve Martin movie, *Trains, Planes and Automobiles*. If you haven't seen it and you travel a lot, rent the movie and watch it. In too many ways, it's not fictional.

This time, the gods had been with me; I made my plane, if just barely. That's when I met the lady in the adjoining seat.

Alley was already buckled in by the time I got to my row. She was a tiny lady; no more than five feet two and maybe—just maybe—105 pounds (good; she didn't take up much space). I excused myself and slipped into the seat next to her.

I was all talked out from the seminar and looking forward to a nice peaceful, *quiet* trip home. Just me and a couple of my favorite car magazines. It doesn't get any better than this. The plane just started to taxi down the runway when my seat partner spoke.

"So you like cars, do you?" she asked, her voice quiet and tentative.

Alley was an attractive younger lady, maybe fifty-five years old or so. She had a certain peace about her. As I was to discover, she was off to see her daughter in Boston. And she wanted—or perhaps, needed—to talk.

"Yes. I love cars."

"David—my husband—always enjoyed cars, too," she said, and so we began.

Although she herself saw cars as nothing more than basic transportation, she went along to the auto shows and to see the new models every year, just to see the excitement on David's face. Not that they could ever afford a new car, what with the bills and all. Even though I would never know the man, how could I already not like him? A car guy with a great name.

Alley had lost David to a heart attack in the middle of the night. They kissed good night, and when she awoke, David was gone forever. We talked a little bit about how at least he hadn't suffered, but I could see this was little solace to a lady who was now left to fend for herself and, as I was to learn, with precious few assets. I was drawn in by Alley's charm and grace. I found myself wanting to know more about this tiny lady.

She and David had been married for just a tad over twenty-five years. In fact, twenty-one days more to be exact. The kids threw them a big silver anniversary party—the best they ever had. All their friends were there. "What still hurts every time I think back to the party were all the plans people were already making for our fiftieth anniversary. Everyone, even the grandkids, was going to meet in Hawaii. We were going to renew our wedding vows. Fifty years. Heck, we never made it to our twenty-sixth."

David and Alley were not rich, at least not financially. David had worked his last twenty years in a surgical supply store, and Alley had put in part-time work as the counter person at a local dry cleaner's. On their meager salaries they had managed to raise three kids, send them all to college, and still put away a few thousand dollars in savings. Little else existed except the $30,000 paid by David's death benefits and the money that was put away each year by their employers in their pension plans.

This was now supposed to be their time. Now it was Alley's time—but she was painfully alone. All three kids had moved away and lived all over the country. Sure, they called and even sent airline tickets for her to fly out and see them occasionally (like today). But life was just not the same—it would never be the same. I had to turn and pretend to look out the window to hide the tears that began to well in my eyes. And to think, all I had wanted to do was sit and read my magazines. Now I only wished there was some way I could help.

That's when she said, "Now that David's gone, I'm rather lost. I don't even know how to plan my own finances."

When the topic came to finances, I was only too glad to give my new friend a little advice. At first, Alley just nodded her head as I talked; when she found out what I do for a living, she began to take notes.

This is essentially what I told her.

Advice Is Never Cheap . . . Unless It's *Bad* Advice

So your last name isn't Rockefeller, Getty, or Gates. So your rich uncle already passed away and you weren't even mentioned in the will. Or maybe your late husband wasn't the fiscal genius he thought he was, and there wasn't all that much left in the will for you when he was gone.

Don't worry. No matter how much or little you presently have on your bottom line, there's still plenty you can do to set up your own financial plan.

Earlier, in chapter 4, I told you what to look for in a good—repeat: *good*—financial advisor. As a result, you know what questions to ask and what type of fee arrangements to expect. But not everybody needs a professional to manage their finances; not everybody wants to share all their financial information with a relative stranger. A few hardy do-it-yourselfers even get a kick out of managing their own money. And if you sign on with anything less than a top-notch advisory—well, quite frankly, in many cases you'd be better off doing it yourself anyway.

However, understand this: No book (not even this one) can possibly teach you to do what takes bona fide financial experts decades to learn. But if you use the same guidelines I do when working with my clients, you'll be surprised at how much you already know. At the very least, you'll get a head start on the correct way to begin analyzing your own personal situation. Certainly, the information below should get you thinking about areas and questions you may not have previously.

A note of warning: If you currently have a broker and he has not gone over all these areas with you *in detail,* find another broker—fast.

Now, let's get started.

You'll need to answer a number of questions in each section, but we'll make it easier by breaking this section into four parts:

Part 1.   How much money do you really need for the rest of your life?
Part 2.   How are you going to create and grow your wealth over time to reach your goals?
Part 3.   How are you going to protect the wealth you have accrued?
Part 4.   How are you going to distribute your estate over time to your heirs with the least amount of taxes and expenses to be paid?

So let's start at the beginning.

Part 1: How Much Do You Really Need for the Rest of Your Life?

Trying to figure out this number is like trying to pick up a handful of mercury: It's hard to corner, let alone get a firm grasp on it. Basically you're looking at three variables:

1.   the amount of money your desired lifestyle will require for each year in retirement before taxes;
2.   your anticipated lifespan; and
3.   the inflation rates and investment-return rates you can reasonably expect.

For instance, if you make $50,000 a year and you're considering retirement next year, several factors come into play. What do you want your average day in retirement to be like? What are your true dreams and desires?

If you're happy to just sit home and watch TV all day, planning is relatively simple. Simply put away enough money to buy a new TV set every six or seven years, calculate the cost of pizza delivery over the foreseeable future, and you're set. (This is, by the way, one of the few scenarios where the average monthly Social Security check may cover the desired lifestyle of a recipient.)

However, most people have higher aspirations. For instance, you may find it may take 60 percent (or more) of your preretirement income to live on if you just plan a relatively Spartan life: hanging around the house, visiting the kids once a year, and maybe taking up watercolor painting as a hobby.

But if you like to play golf, go to the opera, buy a new car every other year, and hope to see the world before you leave it—with these kinds of ambitions, you could easily be looking at 120 percent of your preretirement income, or even more. And if this is as unrealistic for you as it would be for me, it's time to reassess your lifestyle preferences.

If you're still struggling with a lifestyle decision, for our purposes let's just plug in 80 percent of your preretirement income and move on to the next step. Unlike real life, in planning you can always come back and change things.

If you're already retired, this step becomes fairly easy: You *know* what lifestyle you're living. Still, you need to know if it can last.

Part One

Start by going through your checkbook over the last couple of years. Write down headings for each category you come to (utilities, rent/mortgage, insurance, clothes, food, entertainment, etc.) *(See my chart on setting a budget on page 152 for help with filling in all the blanks.)*

Okay. Now you have an idea of how much you will need—but in *today's* dollars; we have to adjust that figure for inflation.

Currently on all financial plans I design I project 3 percent as an annual inflation figure. In practice, this means that if you needed $3,000 a month in your *first* year of retirement, you will need $3,090 the *second,* $3,183 the *third,* and so on. Don't sell yourself short: Go ahead and take your equation out to age ninety-five. See what a difference a few years can make? In the above example, the person who needed $3,000 a month to survive on at age sixty-five would need a whopping *$7,282 a month* at age ninety-five to maintain the same lifestyle.

Investment performance numbers are a little bit trickier, but here is what I do. For all stock-related investments I plug in the figure of 8 percent a year—and this has been a pretty safe bet, because the market actually has returned an average of around 10 percent-plus over the last seventy-five years.

Nonetheless, you must remember two points.

First, this is an *average*. You, and every other investor, will no doubt see many specific years in the future where you will lose money. How much you lose will be dictated by the percentage of money you have in growth-related investments. When you think short-term, any down-market period can be bleak: The more you have in the markets, the more you will lose.

Conversely, it will be the good years that will bring you back in line with that 10-percent average; when the market soars, returns of 20 percent a year and more are not uncommon. Here, obviously the more you have in stocks, the more you will make. Funny how this one works, isn't it? You can think of it as a cosmic balance, but the bottom line is you have to think *long* term if you are going to use these numbers.

Of course, if you're blessed with the gift of prophecy, you can simply be big in stocks when times are good and cash out before the market slumps. But if you think you are that good, give up your day job and move to Wall Street— they need people like you, because they've never had any before.

As for the fixed-income part of the portfolio—bonds, for instance—I currently use 3.5 percent for this figure. Sound low? Actually it is *higher* than the 3.1-percent figure that fixed income has generated on average over the last seventy-five years. Most people are shocked when they hear this, because all they remember is the 16-percent interest rates they received on a six-month CD in the madcap boom market of the early 1980s. Such days are long gone, and only a wild-eyed optimist sees them returning soon.

Now, all you have to do is combine all these numbers, shake (do not stir), and you will get a pretty good idea of where you stand. If you're computer-literate and want even more detail, I suggest you purchase one of the better financial planning programs. Not only will they give you added assistance, all of these programs are spreadsheet-capable; that is, they allow you to play with different numbers and automatically adjust the results and returns you would get with the various figures. They also allow you to update your plan annually or whenever changes in your situation or the market dictate.

Part 2: How Are You Going to Create and Grow Your Wealth Over Time?

Part two of your plan should deal with how you are going to either create this wealth so you can retire in five, ten, or however many years you have until retirement, *or* if you're already retired, invest your dollars in retirement to get the return needed to produce the money you need.

But right here, you need to stop and ask yourself what

I believe is perhaps the most important financial planning question. Certainly, it is one that will affect everything you do from this point forward. Simply, "How much do I need to leave—or *want* to leave—to my children?"

Now, if you own absolutely nothing, the answer is very easy: *nothing*. However, as your estate grows, it is a question that needs to be answered right here and now; your answer will make a huge difference in your financial planning.

Twenty years ago, this was an easy question for me to ask clients. No more. In fact, where almost everyone used to fall into just one category, now *three* distinct categories have emerged, most often determined by the age of the individuals involved. Here's what I mean. Clients react differently to this question based on how they were raised and on their own experiences while growing up. Most of my clients who are seventy-five or older say they want "every last cent" to go to their kids—no matter what, they're determined to leave an estate for their heirs. These people spend nothing but the interest earned on their account, if that. As their parents before them, they would never even consider invading their principal for living expenses. Some are so vehement on this subject, you get the sense that they would rather go search through garbage cans for food late at night than diminish the principal.

Group One: The Depression Generation

Many of these people grew up during the Depression, and those memories scarred them severely. They don't take extended vacations (if they take a vacation at all); the car will have to last another year; and no matter how deteriorated their neighborhood becomes, they simply will not move. They are the same people who will save, save, save for that proverbial rainy day, and it never rains.

And then they die.

Now, this might be a noble gesture—*if* the children or grandchildren they were leaving the money to had their same ideals, and *if* these funds were transferred down from generation to generation. This was the general practice over the previous two hundred years. Unfortunately, times have changed. Today, the odds are good that heirs will spend the money these people hoarded for decades faster than a sailor on leave in Singapore.

Often my clients' adult children sit in on a financial review appointment with their parents; it's a practice that I strongly encourage. But all too often, at some point in the session the children will say, "Go for it, Mom; it's your money, have a good time with it. Spend it *all.*" I've learned through my own disillusioned experience that this often translates to: "I know you'll *never* spend a dime, Mom, but it sure makes you feel good when I say it." Some of the same kids will call me—not infrequently, from the funeral home where Mom is awaiting burial—to ask me about the fastest way to get the money from their late mother's estate.

Group Two: The In-Betweeners

The second category are the in-betweeners; they're probably the most practical and grounded of the three groups. These people, generally fifty-five to seventy-five years old, may like the idea of leaving a large estate to their heirs, but it is not their top priority.

As a group, they tend to have more fun than those who are still reliving the Depression. In-betweeners have no problem buying a new car every so often (typically it's a Buick, even if they could afford a Mercedes). They will take that golfing vacation, maybe even throw in a few private lessons in lieu of watching the latest tournament on TV. They may even book a trip to Las Vegas and allocate a thousand or so dollars to gambling. The point is that they are not afraid to spend money to have fun, but they do it wisely and in moderation.

An example of In-betweener was a fifty-four-year-old client for whom we did a financial plan more than ten years ago. A widow with one adult son, she owned a business that was deteriorating slowly but steadily. It had reached the point where she had a choice: either sink more capital into the business and relocate, or simply close it down.

She had a net worth of approximately $1.4 million, and based on her needs and desires, I assured her we could set up a financial plan she could live on comfortably for the rest of her life.

"There's only one catch," I told her. "I can't project exactly how much money you'll have left in your estate. It could be a lot, or it could be very little."

"Uh-huh," she said, nodding. "Realistically, how soon could I retire?"

I shrugged. "Tomorrow."

Which is precisely what she did, and she's never looked back on her decision. As it turned out, her portfolio has done quite well; she has even more money than she had ten years ago, as well as those extra ten years of retirement.

Group Three: The Grasshoppers

The final group of clients usually ranges in age from twenty to forty-five. For this group, their financial plan is based around quite a simple concept, articulated to me once by a cheerful Grasshopper who was a longtime client.

"David, here's the thing," he said, and winked. "If the check to the undertaker bounces, that's just peachy with me."

With a Grasshopper client, it's a good idea to ask for payment in advance.

The Grasshoppers of the world have no fear. Until recently, they have never seen really bad times and many still live on the assumption that everything will work itself out. No matter what their age, they are too young to think about "old people's" problems. Often, even when advised against it, their portfolios are testaments to a risk-taking philosophy. But even when I can convince them that a more conservative approach is advisable, they expect ready money to be available whenever they ask.

In short, they want it all—*and they want it now.*

Which Fits You?

It's important to know the answer to this question, because it will affect how you perceive wealth. In turn, that will determine how much money you will need to accumulate before you can retire. If you can spend only the interest that your investments earn, you will need either a larger pot of money to pull from, or a willingness to take far more risk on your portfolio than you might otherwise feel comfortable doing.

And maybe both.

If it is okay to spend down some of the principal over time, you will need less money and you can take less risk. If you have no money at retirement, you don't worry about the kids; you're engaged in a day-to-day struggle just to survive.

Now that we have that settled, let's return to creating and growing your wealth. Here you need to examine if the investments you currently have are appropriate to your goals. At the same time, you also must review all those investments you may be considering. There is a yawning gap between that short-term U.S. Government bond fund you hold in your left hand and the small-cap stock fund brochure from the Pacific Rim that you hold in your right. Make sure you get detailed information that will tell you how to evaluate and understand the differences and ramifications of each investment.

And don't forget to examine the tax ramifications. If you are in your late forties or older, and still working, there can be the savings you can achieve, particularly on both high-quality tax-free municipal bonds and tax-deferred annuities. The former offers interest that is federally tax-free, while the latter allows you to invest in the market and have all your growth "tax-deferred" until you pull it out—hopefully, after you retire and are in a lower tax bracket. (There will be a 10-percent penalty on any money earned that you pull out of the contract before age 59½.)

But be careful if you choose this route. Pick a variable annuity only after you've researched the overall quality of the company issuing the annuity contract and compared the different contracts' annual expenses. Everything else being equal, prefer any program with the shortest surrender charges; the ideal situation is a program with none.

Insurance Concerns

In this second category, you also should look at your current insurance program. Don't limit your thinking to life insurance; unfortunately, many people do exactly that, and their first response is "I have enough."

They forget long-term care insurance to help offset costly nursing home bills, disability insurance to guarantee a monthly check if you can no longer work because of illness or injury, health insurance to provide the medical coverage you and your family may need, and umbrella liability insurance policies to cover you for $1 million or more if you ever collide with a bus full of schoolchildren. Here, *all* forms of insurance need to be examined.

Review your auto and homeowners or renters policy every year or so—not only for cost, but for limitation adequacy. A big tip here: *Always* go for the higher amount of auto coverage, but with a higher deductible. I would much rather see my clients have a $500 or $1,000 deductible than a $100 or $250 deductible and then use the savings in premiums to purchase a million-dollar umbrella policy. Certainly, it stings to pay the first thousand dollars the next time you back into a light pole at the mall. But imagine the pain of paying up to *$900,000 more* out of your pocket because you end up on the wrong end of a lawsuit when a four-year-old child darts out in front of your car.

Finally, don't overlook the adequacy of your personal

life insurance policy. Simply stated, first ask yourself whether you need life insurance at all. The premiums for older people tend to be quite high, in any event. If you are seventy-two years old, childless or all your children are married, and you have no one depending on you for their daily support—well, ignore what the nice young insurance salesman tells you (the operative word here is *salesman*). You probably don't need *any* life insurance.

At the other end of the scale, if you are recently widowed and you still have one child in grade school and one in high school, life insurance is a *must,* if there is any way you can afford the premiums. You have to make sure that there will be sufficient funds available to provide for your children's future education, as well as pay off any existing debts you may have.

In my opinion, the best type of insurance to use for this is simple term insurance. You pay only for the insurance you need—not to provide big commissions for the agent or (as with whole-life insurance) to put money away in a side investment fund for future use.

You can usually find term-life insurance sold in level five-, ten-, fifteen-, twenty-, or even thirty-year time frames. This means that the premium you start with will stay the same for the time period you choose. If your children are eight and twelve years old, consider purchasing at least the fifteen-year level-term product. This would provide protection until your last child is out of college. But remember: Nothing is free. The longer the time period you lock into, the higher the annual premium.

If you decide to purchase term insurance, make sure it is automatically renewable (at a higher rate, of course) once your given time period has expired. Imagine: You sign up for the fifteen-year term coverage. Fifteen years and one day later, your health has deteriorated, but because your contract did not give you the option to continue it at a predetermined price, you have no coverage (and won't get it from any other company, at any price).

How Much Insurance Is Enough?

It's a question everyone asks: How much life insurance do you really need?

It's not a simple question to answer.

Many in the insurance industry insist that you should carry life insurance coverage of at least six times your annual salary. By this measure, for instance, if you earn $40,000 a year, you should have approximately $240,000 of life insurance.

This may be a good general rule, and it is clearly better than nothing.

But does this mean that a person earning $1 million a year, with a net worth of $5 million, and no children needs $6 million in life insurance? Hardly. On the other hand, can you tell me someone making $30,000 a year with four kids coming up to the college years needs only $180,000 of life insurance? Ridiculous, and ridiculously underinsured.

Some insurance agents will tell you your life insurance needs are based on what would replace the salary of the dearly departed. That is, if you are making $75,000 a year, you would need to purchase $1.25 million of life insurance. If you die, this money would be invested to generate interest. At a 6-percent rate of return, your family would generate $75,000 a year income and never have to invade the principal. It's not a bad idea—in theory. But a $1.25-million insurance policy is very costly in annual premiums, which is why insurance agents push this scenario so persistently. And of course, inflation would reduce the purchasing power of that $75,000 interest income every year.

The most accurate way of calculating how much life insurance a person really needs is by doing an extensive, in-depth analysis of your expenses, future needs, liabilities, et cetera. Here's how:

a. Add up all your debts. This will include the unpaid mortgage on your house, the balance on your car loan, unpaid future educational needs, burial expenses, unpaid tax liabilities—everything you can think of.

b. List all assets (CDs, stocks, bonds—anything that is reasonably liquid or has a tangible value your heirs could expect to recover). Some people prefer not to include their house here, figuring that the heirs have to live somewhere; others, especially those with grown children who have their own homes, toss it into the asset pile without hesitation.

c. Now, how much money would allow your family to live a decent life, at least till the children are out of college? Let's say the total of the sums of this calculation comes to $1 million.

It is now a case of simple mathematics. Subtract (a) from (b); then subtract that number from (c). You will then have a dollar figure, which is the amount of life insurance you should carry on yourself.

Now you can see what I meant earlier when I said that

some people may not need life insurance at all. If there is no one dependent on you, today or in the future, who are you buying insurance to benefit? If you have a sizable estate with little or no debt, where is the advantage to be gained?

Insurance premiums are expensive and get dramatically more so as the insured ages. At some point, the yearly premium you pay will almost equal the death benefit received. Insurance companies invented the actuarial table, and you cannot beat them at their own game. If you owned the insurance company, what annual premium would you charge a ninety-eight-year-old lady for $50,000 of life insurance?

But this is not to say there are not good reasons to consider life insurance in your planning—that is, if you are already very well off financially. You see, insurance is one of the few remaining areas where you can still help offset the estate tax blues.

Here's a quick example. Let's say you are fifty years old and have an estate of $5 million. Currently, you can leave $1 million after your death to your heirs before estate taxes start to eat into your estate (incidentally, this figure rises to $1.5 million in 2004, $2.0 million in 2006, and $3.5 million in 2009). Using very rough estimations, this means that if the person in this example died tomorrow, her estate would owe approximately $1.5 million in estate taxes, leaving her children a net of $3.5 million. Not bad, but certainly not what she might have envisioned.

Instead, depending on her health, if she purchased a $1.5-million life insurance policy—paying the premium with some of that $1.5 million she was going to give to the government anyway—the insurance payoff would replace what her children would pay to the government in estate taxes. Depending on your health and age, usually under this plan a person will end up paying only 25 to 50 cents on the dollar to settle her estate tax bill—*if* it is set up correctly. Because this is a death benefit, all the proceeds pass on to the heirs free of federal taxes.

Several words of warning here. In my opinion, this is a *great* idea; I use it myself for my own personal estate plan. However, you *must* be absolutely sure you know what you are doing when you set up this type of program. The IRS insists that all the *i*'s be dotted and *t*'s crossed. You might need to set up an insurance trust. You might need to make your children the owners of the policy, so that they pay the annual premium, possibly with funds you gift them yearly. Get expert advice, especially if you plan to do it on your own.

It can get goofy, particularly under the current rollercoaster tax rules. For instance, in 2009 you can leave *$3.5 million* without incurring estate taxes; then, in the year 2010 estate taxes are *repealed altogether,* only to *reappear* in 2011, returning the estate tax–free limit to today's $1 million figure. Crazy? You bet, but it's the law we all have to follow.

Part 3: How Are You Going to Protect the Wealth You Have Accrued?

Let's move on to part three: protecting and preserving the wealth you currently have.

This is where you deal with questions about asset allocation, how to determine what mix of risk is ideal for you, and how taxes play a key role in your overall investment return. We've discussed asset allocation elsewhere in this book, but now it's time to get into the nitty-gritty.

Don't fear. Asset allocation is no more than the lesson mothers have taught their children for generations: *Don't put all your eggs in one basket.* But how many baskets do we really need? A lot of little ones or one big one? Should they all be the same size? Does color matter?

In my practice, I start each client off in one of five different basic portfolio models. Where any given client fits is based upon her answers from a long list of questions—her age, how she feels about risk, her present financial situation, and how much money she will need to retire happily. The categories are:

1. Income with capital preservation (80/20),
2. Income with moderate growth (60/40),
3. Growth with income (40/60),
4. Growth (20/80),
5. Aggressive growth (5/95).

Notice the numbers inside the parentheses. The first number represents the percentage of money of the entire portfolio that should be placed in *fixed income* such as CDs, cash, money markets, bonds, et cetera. The second number represents the percentage of your portfolio that should have individual stocks, stock-related mutual funds, real estate trusts, or other *growth-related* investments.

Here's where the process gets a little more complicated. Let's say you decide you're most suited to the "income with moderate growth" portfolio. Great. You now know that you feel comfortable with 60 percent of your investable assets in fixed income and 40 percent in growth-related ventures. But *which* fixed-income and *which* growth vehicles should you purchase? Do you just put 60 percent of your money in a six-month CD, buy Microsoft with the other 40 percent, and call it a day?

I think not.

The money you put on the fixed side needs to be spread out among short-term (one to three years in duration), intermediate-term (three to ten years in duration), and long-term (ten to thirty years in duration) fixed-income vehicles. In addition, you need to divide the money between high-, intermediate-, and low-quality fixed investments. There are a number of companies that carefully examine the quality of the bond—I use Morningstar—and rate the bond from AAA (the best) down through the alphabet.

In general, AAA-quality bonds will pay you less than AA, A, BBB, or lower-letter investments. It's a matter of risk: The better the quality of the bond you buy, the more likely you are to get 100 percent of your money back when the bond matures five years, ten years, or even thirty years down the road. As a result, they can get away with paying you less interest. This is precisely why CDs are among the lowest-paying fixed investments around; because they're backed by FDIC insurance, the risk is low.

So why buy *any* low-quality bonds? Because usually the greater the risk, the greater the reward. It is not unusual to find these so-called *junk bonds* paying you 3 percent or 4 percent more interest each year. Many investors simply can't resist the temptation.

That's exactly the reason why U.S. Treasuries are *al-*

ways among the lowest interest-paying bonds around. With Treasury bonds, the odds are really, *really* good that every investor will get their money back in the future. If the U.S. government ever defaults on its debt, the only thing left for any of us may be to plant tomato seeds amid the ruins of what would be our once-great civilization. And pray for rain.

The Hazards of Fixed-Income Vehicles

Here's a point you *must* understand about fixed-income investments: If you need to cash your bonds in early, there are repercussions. The further from the bond's maturity date, or the more the interest rate has moved (up *or* down) from the original interest rate when the bond was issued, the more your profit or loss will be if you sell that bond prematurely.

Pay very close attention here, because when I ask potential clients about early withdrawals, a whopping *95 percent of them get this answer wrong*. This figure includes people who already have these types of investments in their portfolios.

Let's say you purchase a hypothetical twenty-year bond today at 6-percent interest and you invest $25,000. This just means that the bond guarantees to pay you 6-percent interest annually for the next twenty years, usually in semiannual payments (you would get a check for $750 every six months for the next twenty years). It will return your original $25,000 investment to you at the end of the twenty-year term. And that's it—not a penny more, not a penny less.

When you purchased the bond, the deal was that you don't get the money back for the twenty-year period. But things happen, and let's just assume you needed the cash for an emergency early. Fifteen years early, to be exact. Instead of the 6-percent interest that was being paid when you bought the bond, let's speculate that fifteen-year interest rates are at 8 percent when you cashed it today.

What happens to your principal?

To sell a bond, you must find someone who wants to buy it. But no one will want to buy your 6-percent-paying bond when the going interest rate today is 8 percent.

So what happens? You have to discount your bond.

You may only get $20,000 or so for the bond that originally cost you $25,000. You lose $5,000. At the same time, the purchaser of your bond will continue to get the 6-percent annual income for the next fifteen years, but at maturity he can redeem the bond for the full $25,000. The "extra" $5,000 brings his total return to 8 percent a year—and everything comes out even.

Of course, in the above circumstances you would have *made* a little money if interest rates had *dropped* to 4 percent rather than rising. In this case the new buyer must pay *you* a premium to buy your bond—perhaps $30,000 for the $25,000 you originally invested—and you gain $5,000. The purchaser will receive the 6-percent interest for the next fifteen years, but he will get only $25,000 back for the bond at maturity. Thus, with the loss of principal, he will receive an overall annual return of just 4 percent.

Sometimes buying long-term bonds can be an investment strategy in itself. Often I will buy twenty- to thirty-year Treasury bonds for some of my more astute clients. This is when I believe interest rates are high, and I think rates on these particular bonds may come down in the future.

In such a situation, I have no intention of holding the bond for twenty or thirty years. In fact, we may own them for only several months. When rates come down, I sell the bonds, put the money in the money market, and wait for interest rates to go up again so we can do the whole process again. When things go in our favor, we can see total returns of 10 percent or more a year using U.S. Treasuries instead of stocks.

What if rates go *up* instead? In that case, I simply wait for the rates to change back in my favor. All the while, my clients are collecting a modest rate of interest in a safe vehicle that is backed by the full faith and credit of the U.S. government.

A warning: This strategy is not for everyone. It's definitely not something on which to risk all your investable assets or even all your investable fixed-income assets. You must know the ins and outs of this strategy before attempting it on your own, or you can be burned badly.

Now let's look at the other side of your portfolio's equation: the growth segment.

The "Investment" Side

If fixed income is complicated, it's child's play compared to the "invest for growth" segment, the one that involves 40 percent of your total portfolio in this model.

Here, we divide the pie into twelve sections, for such vehicles as large-cap growth stocks, mid-cap blend stocks, small-cap value stocks, international/world holdings—and everything in between.

Now, don't panic if you don't know what these terms

mean. These are pretty sophisticated for the average person, but your investment advisor will be happy to explain each in detail. For now, if you really want a definition, I've provided a glossary at the back of this book.

Usually, I will fill these categories with managed mutual funds and index funds. In some models, we may have up to 50 percent of the growth investable assets dedicated to the large-cap sector, while small-caps may get only 15 percent and international only 10 percent. Why? Small-cap stocks and international holdings are usually much more volatile than large-cap holdings. For that reason, they get the lower weightings. But with volatility often comes opportunity, so don't overlook these categories out of fear. The trick is to balance—to make sure that each category is set up to meet your needs.

How do you decide how much of the 40 percent goes into each section of the pie? Clearly, it is not a matter of simply dividing 40 by 12 and putting 3.3 percent of your money into each category.

Professionals use formulas that tell us exactly how to proceed, based on each client's particular circumstances. I could easily spend the next hundred pages going through dust-dry formulas and calculations that *might* make sense to you—if you chose to read them at all.

Instead, here are four steps to help you deal with asset allocation—*before* you invest any of your money.

1. Visit your local library or bookstore and pick up a couple of books that are solely dedicated to the topic of asset allocation and its goals and principles. Read them and edu-

cate yourself to the point you feel comfortable handling your own account.

2.   Go to your local library and ask to see all the information they have on Morningstar Mutual Funds. You will find they have a great deal of information on how mutual funds operate and how to pick the best of the best mutual funds available in each category.

3.   Get all the books, read them, and then visit the wealth of information on the Internet on these topics. You may even find ready-made asset-allocation plans depending on your age and goals that will help guide you step by step.

4.   Once you think you have become an expert in the field, get a second opinion before you invest. Find a fee-based financial advisor and have him review your plan for accuracy and content. It will be well worth the few hundred dollars he or she will charge you to know you're on the right road. Remember: This is your future and you may get only one shot at it.

A final word about asset allocation. No matter how good your asset-allocation plan, if you constantly withdraw more money than you make, you risk major trouble down the road. Remember: You must remain committed to your goal and look at the bigger picture to ensure you don't outlive your money.

Part 4: How Are You Going to Distribute Your Estate?

How do you distribute your estate to your heirs over time with the least amount of taxes and expenses due? First of all, let's take a closer look at exactly what an estate really is. I grew up thinking for most of my childhood that an estate was a large house in the best of neighborhoods that sat on about ten acres of land with an in-ground swimming pool.

Today I know better. It needs at least twenty-five acres to be considered an estate.

All joking aside, serious estate planning is no longer just for the rich and famous. Your personal estate is made up of all the assets you have accumulated over your lifetime. They include your real estate, bank accounts, stocks, bonds, mutual funds, automobiles—everything you own, right down to the good silverware. It doesn't matter if the total value of your estate is $25,000 or $25 million, good estate planning will save your heirs in taxes, in lawyer's fees, and in every type of related expense. This is not to mention all the possible headaches and family fights you could help avoid when you are gone.

Still, with all this in the balance, *less than 50 percent of all people set up estate plans.*

And it's mainly due to fear, specifically the fear that all of us share about death. Nobody likes to talk about death, especially their own. It's as if we assume that if we don't talk about it, the Grim Reaper will pass us by.

However, there is a tranquillity that comes from dealing with this inevitability. I've noticed it with my clients:

When the process is finished, it is as if a tremendous burden has been lifted from their shoulders. And why not? Facing your fears always makes a difference—to *everyone*.

When I arrived home, I didn't even look at the mail for two days—it could wait. All I wanted to do was spend time with my family. For that feeling, I thank Alley, and hope somehow what I had to say to her that day helped her get on with her life.

BUDGET FOR RETIREMENT WORKSHEET

Sources of Income $		Expenses $	
Former employer benefit plan (includes pensions and profit sharing)	$	Rent or monthly mortgage payments	$
IRA withdrawals	$	Food	$
Net income from real estate	$	Medical, including insurance premiums	$
Social Security	$	Local travel	$
Dividend income from stocks	$	Vacation travel and hotels	$
Interest from banks, bonds, mortgages	$	Entertainment (theater, movies, home, etc.)	$
Income from part-time work	$	Newspapers, magazine subscriptions	$
Annuities: A	$	Gifts	$
B	$	Charitable contributions	$
C	$	Automobile expenses	$
D	$	Property and other insurance	$
E	$	Alimony and/or child support	$
Other	$	Membership dues	$
		Domestic help or home care	$
		Home maintenance	$
		Other	$
Total Income	$	Total Expenses	$

RETIREMENT EXPENSE WORKSHEET

	Estimated Current Expenses	Retirement Expenses (Today's $)	Increasing Expense?	
Contributions	$_____	$_____		
Home				
Mortgage	$_____	$_____	Yes	No
Insurance	$_____	$_____	Yes	No
Real estate taxes	$_____	$_____	Yes	No
Maintenance/repairs	$_____	$_____	Yes	No
Utilities				
Electric/gas/water	$_____	$_____	Yes	No
Phone (including toll charges)	$_____	$_____	Yes	No
Cable TV	$_____	$_____	Yes	No
Security system	$_____	$_____	Yes	No
Insurance				
Medical	$_____	$_____	Yes	No
Personal Care (prescriptions, etc.)	$_____	$_____	Yes	No
Homeowners	$_____	$_____	Yes	No
Auto	$_____	$_____	Yes	No
Long-term Care	$_____	$_____	Yes	No
Children				
Clothing	$_____	$_____	Yes	No
School tuition/expenses	$_____	$_____	Yes	No
Gifts	$_____	$_____	Yes	No
Other	$_____	$_____	Yes	No
Debt Payments				
Autos	$_____	$_____	Yes	No
Personal loans	$_____	$_____	Yes	No
Income taxes	$_____	$_____	Yes	No
Other	$_____	$_____	Yes	No
Total	$_____	$_____	Yes	No

Ten Considerations for Your Estate Planning

1.   **Percentages Rule.** Always use percentages rather than dollar amounts when talking about how much money you are going to leave someone in your will or trust. What if you won $10 million in the lottery just before you died? You left your son $10,000—because that is all you had at the time you wrote your will. What happens to the rest? It goes to probate court to have a judge decide.

2.   **Name All Names.** Always name anyone directly in your will or trust that you think might cause trouble or contest your will or trust after you die. Simply stating "to my nephew George I leave the grand sum of $1.00 and the best of luck" will tell a probate judge what your true intentions were. If you don't say it, someone may think they were left out by accident.

3.   **State Your Preferences.** It's okay to treat your children differently when it comes to their inheritance. You don't have to divide everything equally. Can you leave more to the child who helped you every day in retirement till the day you died instead of the one who lives two thousand miles away and called you only on Christmas and Easter? Not only can you, why wouldn't you? Paternal instinct may tell you to leave more to your severely disabled child and less to your successful tycoon. But instinct is wrong here. The government will provide for your severely disabled child *after the money you provided is depleted.* Thus, in this case, your well-intended gift would be in vain.

4.   **Anticipate Interfamily Quarrels.** If you have four children, you don't have to, nor do you want to, name them all as

co-executors of your estate. Choose the child in this case who has the most financial savvy, lives close by, and can be trusted to do the long, tedious job of distributing your estate.

5.   **Death and Taxes.** Every estate will have certain expenses or taxes that must be paid in a timely manner. Make sure you leave enough money liquid for your estate to pay these bills. If it is a rather large estate, you might even name the assets you would like to see sold to cover these costs. Don't expect your executor to be a mind reader.

6.   **Tie up all the Loose Ends.** Make a list for your executor and check it twice as to where and who to call about all items in your estate. Things that you may know off the top of your head may take someone else unfamiliar with the situation days or weeks to piece together.

7.   **Explain It All.** Leave detailed instructions and comments about *why* you did the things you did in your will or trust. Especially if things look a little lopsided in favor of one child or another. This will hopefully not leave one child forever asking, "Why did Mom leave things that way?" Maybe it's because he called only on Christmas and Easter; I don't know. But if it is—tell them. You don't want your heirs to be tortured by words that can be construed as hurtful or angry. Be diplomatic and sensitive if you can, but be clear. It's kinder in the long run.

8.   **Think Charitable Thoughts.** What charities do you want to support? Do you want them to get your money directly or as a pool of money? If it is a relatively small amount of money, have it paid directly to them in one lump sum. For larger sums, I am in favor of going the pool-of-money route. This means that the money you leave them will go into a pool of money to be paid out quarterly, annually, or on some other schedule. If it is a very large sum of money, you can name your child or some-

one else to manage the pool and collect a salary every year for doing so.

9.   **To Heir Is Human.** How much money do you really want to leave your children? Opinions vary here from "every last red cent" to what financial guru Warren Buffett said: "Enough money so that they feel they could do anything, but not so much that they could do nothing." The choice is yours. It's your money and you can do as you wish. After all, you know your children's strengths and weaknesses.

10. **Gift Them Today.** Don't be afraid to gift your children or any other heir money *today*—instead of at your death—especially if you can afford to do so. Currently you can gift *anyone* up to $11,000 in any and every given calendar year without any gift taxes owed on your gift. Unfortunately, every year I will get calls from clients asking how they write this gift off on their taxes. Get this straight: Not only do you *not* get to write off the gift to your heir, you as the giver will have to pay a gift tax if the amount you give goes beyond $11,000 to any single individual in any calendar year. Why give it now instead of at death? Because that money given today while they are younger and struggling may mean more to them now than ten times that amount later when they may not need it.

Ten Cardinal Rules of Investing

1.   **Never borrow against your house to buy growth-related investments.** Inevitably, someone will tell you this is a smart idea: Why not use all that idle equity sitting there in your

home to build wealth? Answer: because it's too easy to lose it in a bad market.

2. **Never use margin.** Margin is simply borrowing against your securities to buy more securities. This is great in a bull market, but it means you will lose twice as fast on the way down, and you will get the notorious "margin call" request. Leave this strictly to the professionals. To get a comical look at what a margin call can do for you, rent the old Eddie Murphy movie *Trading Places*.

3. **If you are still working and not yet retired, always make sure you pay yourself first.** This just means whenever you set up a budget, make sure you have a category for monthly deposits into your investment account. Also make sure this category comes ahead of new car, clothes, and entertainment in priority. If you don't pay yourself first, trust me, it'll never get done.

4. **Be patient for the long term.** Americans are among the most impatient people in the world when it comes to investing. Most people view long term as three months—not ten years. Make a plan, stick to it, and change it only because your goals or situation has changed—not because the market didn't do what you wanted it to last week.

5. **Never go into credit card debt.** There is absolutely no reason in the world to create a debt that you are going to pay 18 percent a year interest on. The only exception is food (and I don't mean caviar). If you are going into debt this way—you're living well beyond your means. Stop it immediately.

6. **Always use asset allocation in your investments.** It is estimated that over 90 percent of the time people make money in the markets because of asset allocation. Timing the market is only 3 percent.

7. Rebalance your portfolio once a year. Why? Several reasons. Over time the investment percentages you started with will slowly get out of whack, and you need to bring them back in balance to what you started with. Also, your goals may have changed over the last year. This may be the year you retire, you remarry, your Aunt Martha passes away and leaves everything to you, you have a major health problem, or you're just not satisfied with how your portfolio has been performing. However, always take tax implications into account in any rebalancing you do.

8. Educate yourself. If you are gung-ho about doing it on your own terms, take it seriously. Don't read one magazine article or listen to some tape and end your education there. Financial knowledge takes time to acquire. I have to go through continuing education every year to keep up on new trends and ideas to keep my license; you should do the same if you are going to run your own show. People will spend more time planning a two-week vacation than they will their entire financial future.

9. Make sure your will or living trust is up to date and accurate. You can try to do this yourself also—but when you are finished, at least have an attorney who specializes in these matters review it for accuracy and content. Remember: You may not be around or able to answer questions when the time comes to ask them.

10. Always read the fine print. It's seldom the big print that will hurt you; it's the little stuff you never read. If the investment sounds too complicated to you—walk away. Never invest your money in things you don't understand.

Ten Guidelines for Your Financial Planning

1. **Don't forget about inflation.** Often people ask me to review their plans for the future. In a surprising number of instances, they totally forget to figure inflation into their calculations. Depending on the rate you ultimately use, you could easily see things double or even triple in price during your retirement years. A good benchmark would be 3 percent a year.

2. **Always run your life expectancy calculations out to age ninety-five.** Unless you face an extraordinary health-related situation, you're not going to be very happy at age eighty when you run out of money because you didn't plan accordingly. Better to have a little left over than not enough.

3. **Make sure you have the correct type and amount of insurance coverage.** This includes life, health, disability, long-term care, liability, homeowners/renters, auto, etc. Review each of them often for cost and appropriateness.

4. **Make sure you have a durable power of attorney.** Do this not only for your financial affairs but also to deal with any health-care issues. This will ensure there is an orderly plan in place for managing your affairs if you cannot or no longer desire to do so. If you don't decide it now, the courts will later. Same goes for health care. Do you want to be strapped up to a machine for the last months—or even years—of your life? If not, do something about it now.

5. **Don't let greed overcome you.** No matter how good a financial guru you think you are, never put more than 10 percent of your investable assets in any single stock or investment. Always remember the Enron investors.

6. Don't forget to add in taxes to any plan you design. Uncle Sam will still want his share if you are retired or not. This includes all his nephews and nieces at the state and local levels, too. Depending on the state you live in and the amount of money you need to live on each year, you may have to add as much as 40 percent more to your earnings just to pay federal, state, county, property, sales, Social Security, and Medicare taxes. The taxman never sleeps.

7. Be realistic. Hopefully, you now know how much money you need to live the retirement lifestyle you want. Can you achieve this goal by only withdrawing 3 percent of your account each year, in addition to any Social Security or pension income? If so, great; you are on the right path. This is a good general rule in all financial planning. The more money you can leave untouched in your account, the more money there is to continue growing. If you can actually live on the figure you've calculated, you will live better for longer. Certainly, that will make your retirement years much more enjoyable.

8. Never purchase a mutual fund during the last quarter of the year in a taxable account until the fund makes its year-end distribution. This rule especially baffles investors. Because of current tax laws, mutual funds are required to distribute income and capital gains to investors at least once a year. Most companies wait until December to do this. That means if you buy the fund in November, you will actually be paying taxes on the fund as if you owned it the entire year. Unless there is some compelling underlying reason to buy the fund anyway, always wait till the distribution is paid.

9. Be patient and plan for the long term. It isn't *timing* the market that counts—it's *time in* the market that will usually give you your best results.

10. Be skeptical of all advice, particularly when your action will benefit a second party. Don't believe everything you hear and believe only half of what you see.

Three Tips on Picking a Good Insurance Policy

1. **Don't automatically pick the cheapest contract.** It may very well be the best deal, but make sure you are comparing apples to apples. Policies can vary greatly.

2. **Always check the ratings of the insurance company.** Just as individual bonds are rated for their quality, so are insurance companies. A. M. Best, Standard & Poor's, Moody's, Duff & Phelps, and Weiss are five of the top rating companies for insurance companies. (Note: *Always* ask for the ratings of the company you are considering. *Never* purchase a contract that has a rating from any of these rating companies that is more than three notches from the top of the scale used by any of the rating agencies. Remember: Your contract is only as good as the company's ability to pay your claim. *(See "How Insurance Companies Are Ranked" on page 89.)*

3. **Never cancel an old policy until you have received your new policy in your hand.** It may be tempting to save a few dollars by canceling your old contract as soon as you apply for new insurance. But what if the new company turns you down for coverage because they find that cough you have is more than a cough? Or, even worse, what if you were in a car accident and died before your new policy was issued?

Games Brokers Play: An Update

Merrill Settles with New York Attorney General*

ALBANY, N.Y. (May 21, 2002)—Merrill Lynch & Co. agreed to pay $100 million to settle allegations that the firm's analysts misled investors with their stock ratings so the company could win lucrative investment banking fees.

Merrill Lynch said Tuesday it will make the payment to New York State, which has been investigating the matter, and to all the other states provided they all accept it.

The nation's biggest brokerage firm agreed to structural reforms to assure that its stock analysts work independently from the firm's investment bankers who do business with some of the same companies. The firm also apologized.

"This agreement changes the way Wall Street will operate, severing the compensation link between the research and banking divisions that tainted investment advice," New York State Attorney General Eliot Spitzer told a news conference.

Under the settlement, Merrill Lynch analysts will no longer be paid with money generated by the firm's investment banking business.

A chief concern of critics has been that analysts have been rewarded for the investment banking business they bring in instead of having compensation tied to the quality of their stock research.

Developing Your Financial Plan

Using the Money Growth Rate Factor Table

The Money Growth Rate Factor Table (see page 165) is a useful tool for determining the growth you can expect based on the annual interest you can earn for the amount of money you have available to invest. Of course, the chart is cumulative; it's only accurate if you leave the money *untouched* in the account until retirement.

Here's how to use it:

1. Go down the left column and pick the desired number of years until retirement.
2. Move right to your expected rate of return on your investment.
3. Multiply the amount of money you now have by this factor. This will tell you the amount of money you will have the day you retire.

Major Points

Remember: These numbers do not take into consideration any federal or state taxes that need to be paid as you go.

Play with the numbers. See how your totals come out using different percentages over time. For example, $100,000 over twelve years at 4 percent becomes $160,000, while that same amount over that same time period at 8 percent becomes $252,000.

Pick only a portfolio that you can live with. Do not get so aggressive that when the market goes down (and it has and it will again) you cannot take the pressure and start to sell. Instead, pick the portfolio that you can live with on the way down as well as on the way up.

MONEY GROWTH RATE FACTOR TABLE

Years Until Retirement	Expected Return on Investment												
1	1.03	1.04	1.05	1.06	1.07	1.08	1.09	1.10	1.11	1.12	1.13	1.14	1.15
2	1.06	1.08	1.10	1.12	1.14	1.17	1.19	1.21	1.23	1.25	1.28	1.30	1.32
3	1.09	1.12	1.16	1.19	1.23	1.26	1.30	1.33	1.37	1.40	1.44	1.48	1.52
4	1.13	1.17	1.22	1.26	1.31	1.36	1.41	1.46	1.52	1.57	1.63	1.69	1.75
5	1.16	1.22	1.28	1.34	1.40	1.47	1.54	1.61	1.69	1.76	1.84	1.93	2.01
6	1.19	1.27	1.34	1.42	1.50	1.59	1.68	1.77	1.87	1.97	2.08	2.19	2.31
7	1.23	1.32	1.41	1.50	1.61	1.71	1.83	1.95	2.08	2.21	2.35	2.50	2.66
8	1.27	1.37	1.48	1.59	1.72	1.85	1.99	2.14	2.30	2.48	2.66	2.85	3.06
9	1.30	1.42	1.55	1.69	1.84	2.00	2.17	2.36	2.56	2.77	3.00	3.25	3.52
10	1.34	1.48	1.63	1.79	1.97	2.16	2.37	2.59	2.84	3.11	3.39	3.71	4.05
11	1.38	1.54	1.71	1.90	2.10	2.33	2.58	2.85	3.15	3.48	3.84	4.23	4.65
12	1.43	1.60	1.80	2.01	2.25	2.52	2.81	3.14	3.50	3.90	4.33	4.82	5.35
13	1.47	1.67	1.89	2.13	2.41	2.72	3.07	3.45	3.88	4.36	4.90	5.49	6.15
14	1.51	1.73	1.98	2.26	2.58	2.94	3.34	3.80	4.31	4.89	5.53	6.26	7.08
15	1.56	1.80	2.08	2.40	2.76	3.17	3.64	4.18	4.78	5.47	6.25	7.14	8.14
16	1.60	1.87	2.18	2.54	2.95	3.43	3.97	4.59	5.31	6.13	7.07	8.14	9.36
17	1.65	1.95	2.29	2.69	3.16	3.70	4.33	5.05	5.90	6.87	7.99	9.28	10.76
18	1.70	2.03	2.41	2.85	3.38	4.00	4.72	5.56	6.54	7.69	9.02	10.58	12.38
19	1.75	2.11	2.53	3.03	3.62	4.32	5.14	6.12	7.26	8.61	10.20	12.06	14.23
20	1.81	2.19	2.65	3.21	3.87	4.66	5.60	6.73	8.06	9.65	11.52	13.74	16.37
21	1.86	2.28	2.79	3.40	4.14	5.03	6.11	7.40	8.95	10.80	13.02	15.67	18.82
22	1.92	2.37	2.93	3.60	4.43	5.44	6.66	8.14	9.93	12.10	14.71	17.86	21.64
23	1.97	2.46	3.07	3.82	4.74	5.87	7.26	8.95	11.03	13.55	16.63	20.36	24.89
24	2.03	2.56	3.23	4.05	5.07	6.34	7.91	9.85	12.24	15.18	18.79	23.21	28.63
25	2.09	2.67	3.39	4.29	5.43	6.85	8.62	10.83	13.59	17.00	21.23	26.46	32.92
26	2.16	2.78	3.56	4.55	5.81	7.40	9.40	11.92	15.08	19.04	23.99	30.17	37.86
27	2.22	2.88	3.73	4.82	6.21	7.99	10.25	13.11	16.74	21.32	27.11	34.39	43.54
28	2.29	3.00	3.92	5.11	6.65	8.63	11.17	14.42	18.58	23.88	30.63	39.20	50.07
29	2.36	3.12	4.12	5.42	7.11	9.32	12.17	15.86	20.62	26.75	34.62	44.69	57.58
30	2.43	3.24	4.32	5.74	7.61	10.06	13.27	17.45	22.89	29.96	39.12	50.95	66.21
	3%	4%	5%	6%	7%	8%	9%	10%	11%	12%	13%	14%	15%

INFLATION MULTIPLIER TABLE

Years Until Retirement	Estimated Inflation Rate							
	1%	2%	3%	4%	5%	6%	7%	8%
1	1.01	1.02	1.03	1.04	1.05	1.06	1.07	1.08
2	1.02	1.04	1.06	1.08	1.10	1.12	1.14	1.17
3	1.03	1.06	1.09	1.12	1.16	1.19	1.23	1.26
4	1.04	1.08	1.13	1.17	1.22	1.26	1.31	1.36
5	1.05	1.10	1.16	1.22	1.28	1.34	1.40	1.47
6	1.06	1.13	1.19	1.27	1.34	1.42	1.50	1.59
7	1.07	1.15	1.23	1.32	1.41	1.50	1.61	1.71
8	1.08	1.17	1.27	1.37	1.48	1.59	1.72	1.85
9	1.09	1.20	1.30	1.42	1.55	1.69	1.84	2.00
10	1.10	1.22	1.34	1.48	1.63	1.79	1.97	2.16
11	1.12	1.24	1.38	1.54	1.71	1.90	2.10	2.33
12	1.13	1.27	1.43	1.60	1.80	2.01	2.25	2.52
13	1.14	1.29	1.47	1.67	1.89	2.13	2.41	2.72
14	1.15	1.32	1.51	1.73	1.98	2.26	2.58	2.94
15	1.16	1.35	1.56	1.80	2.08	2.40	2.76	3.17
16	1.17	1.37	1.60	1.87	2.18	2.54	2.95	3.43
17	1.18	1.40	1.65	1.95	2.29	2.69	3.16	3.70
18	1.20	1.43	1.70	2.03	2.41	2.85	3.38	4.00
19	1.21	1.46	1.75	2.11	2.53	3.03	3.62	4.32
20	1.22	1.49	1.81	2.19	2.65	3.21	3.87	4.66
21	1.23	1.52	1.86	2.28	2.79	3.40	4.14	5.03
22	1.24	1.55	1.92	2.37	2.93	3.60	4.43	5.44
23	1.26	1.58	1.97	2.46	3.07	3.82	4.74	5.87
24	1.27	1.61	2.03	2.56	3.23	4.05	5.07	6.34
25	1.28	1.64	2.09	2.67	3.39	4.29	5.43	6.85
26	1.30	1.67	2.16	2.77	3.56	4.55	5.81	7.40
27	1.31	1.71	2.22	2.88	3.73	4.82	6.21	7.99
28	1.32	1.74	2.29	3.00	3.92	5.11	6.65	8.63
29	1.33	1.78	2.36	3.12	4.12	5.42	7.11	9.32
30	1.35	1.81	2.43	3.24	4.32	5.74	7.61	10.06

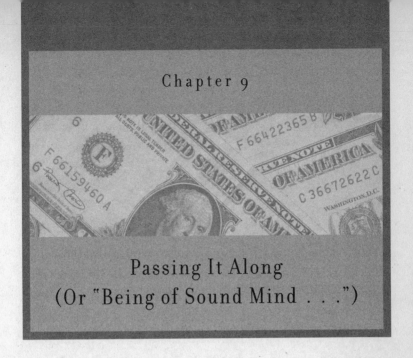

Chapter 9

Passing It Along
(Or "Being of Sound Mind . . .")

When it comes to money, stocks and bonds, real estate, and all the other property that comprise what the legal profession terms your "estate," the oldest adage is still the most true: You really can't take it with you.

But you can sure leave a mess behind when you go—especially if that is exactly what you intended to do.

And that's how I'd like to introduce you to my client, Tom. But I can't, because he's dead.

Tom, by all evidence, intended to spend eternity laughing himself sick—that is, if such a thing is permitted from wherever Tom is spending his final reward.

When he came in to see me, Tom made no secret of his personal philosophy, developed over his sixty-four years on this earth. For Tom, the world was a tough place; you survived by looking out for yourself. In fact, I still remember one of the first questions Tom asked me.

"So," he said, smiling to take the sting from his words, "I'm curious. How are you going to get your hand in my pocket and put my money in yours?"

He was not, to put it mildly, the most trusting man I have met.

Physically, he was one of the most impressive: six feet four, probably two hundred and fifty pounds. In many ways, he still looked like the young man who went to college on a football scholarship; certainly, he still had the self-confidence of the top-notch athlete. He was a very big man, and he had very big opinions. To be fair, however, Tom had probably earned the right to his opinions. In college, he already knew he didn't want to work for somebody else; he learned early that owning your own business was the way to accrue true wealth. He trusted his instincts and abilities, and started a string of automobile part stores that did very well. When I met Tom and his wife Julie, they had a net worth of slightly over $2 million.

The problem wasn't that Tom did not *trust* me; he was my client for seven years, and as we grew to know each other, it became obvious that he did. The big problem was he didn't *listen* to me.

My professional relationship with Tom was . . . well, unusual. For the first couple of years, Tom seemed to be testing me. He'd call, just to see if I would call him back. He would ask for a special report or some research, just to see if my client service was what I said it would be. He would solicit investment advice, just to see if what I predicted actually came true. But he never actually acted on the research or followed the advice. It was maddening, and several times I made the decision that the time I spent on Tom could be better used to help other clients. I would wish Tom and Julie well, and figure that was that.

But it never was; I never carried through with it.

I'm sure the reason I kept the couple as clients through the years was because of Julie. Julie was the same age as Tom, but she always seemed to be a little bit in awe of her husband. He would tell her, in general terms, what he intended to do; she would nod her head and concur.

Even now, I don't believe it was because she didn't care, or didn't want to know, or couldn't understand financial information. I'm convinced that she just felt comfortable letting Tom handle it all. And why not? There was always enough money for her to spend. She never needed to balance a checkbook. She knew that she could use her credit cards. She knew that Tom always made sure there was money to pay the bills. For Julie, to all outward appearances, it was a relatively easy life.

But there were hints that she realized it might not always be that way. Occasionally, after a meeting with the two of them when Tom had once again ignored some important bit of advice, I would get a call from Julie on her car phone, apologizing, smoothing the waters, urging patience, and tacitly asking that I keep them on my client list. Mainly because of her efforts, I did.

And then last year Tom passed away.

He went out, fittingly enough, on the playing field. On the seventh hole, Tom hit a long drive that sliced off into the woods. He banged his club against the ground, threw it in his bag, and keeled over two steps from the tee.

It was a massive stroke. Tom lingered in the intensive care unit for five days, never regaining consciousness. In a sense, Tom was lucky; had he lived, he would have been in a vegetative state. As it turned out, Julie was lucky too—but for an entirely different reason. But that was later.

"Oh, people thought we had the perfect life, I'm sure," Julie recalls now. "We had the right house, took the right vacations, drove the right cars. Tom even died in the 'right' way—no lingering illness, no wasting away, no untidy mess." She stops, and her voice carries just a touch of bitterness. "All the mess. Well, that came afterward."

Underneath this American dream that they had lived in public, Tom and Julie had a lot of family problems. Most of the trouble seemed to center around their three adult sons, Mark, David, and Joseph. Mark never finished college; he just never could seem to get his act together. He married, bounced around a few jobs for a few years. Finally, he and his wife moved away, citing "interference" from Tom and Julie as the heart of their many problems. Tom and Julie rarely heard from Mark except when he needed money.

David, the middle son, at least made it into college—only to end up with a drug problem. It was a not-uncommon tale of arrests and jail time intermingled with various rehab programs (paid for, of course, by Tom and Julie) to get David on the right course. Nothing seemed to work; finally, they gave up. For the two years prior to Tom's death, they had no word from David.

Joseph, the youngest son, still lived in the area. While he had regular contact with Tom and Julie, Joseph had more than his share of problems. At the time of Tom's death,

Joseph was already into his third marriage, with three children by two different ex-wives and yet another child living with him now. Did I mention he had a drinking problem?

I mention all this about the kids because this is really the genesis of the time bomb Tom left Julie.

Much of what I do for clients is to provide estate planning assistance. Sometimes this is simple; it is a matter of organizing their assets and arranging the holdings to minimize taxes, probate problems, and related headaches that can plague the survivors.

There are really three elements to estate planning. In the case of a husband and wife, the most important is to ensure that there is enough for the surviving spouse to live on. On the face of it, Tom had done very well in this area. There were assets in excess of $2.4 million, and on that Julie could live comfortably for the balance of her life.

The second part of estate planning is to arrange everything so that what you have actually goes to the individual you want it to go to. I'm certain that Tom wanted everything to go to his wife. But this did not happen.

Tom and Julie had done some planning. For instance, from day one of their marriage, they had always split all their assets: Half of everything was in Tom's name, and the other half in Julie's. That gave each partner comfort about their future, as well as a net worth of about $1.2 million each at the time of Tom's death.

For years, I urged Tom to show me the will he said he had written and to work with me to plan his estate. All to no avail; I could not understand his inaction. Finally, I must have pushed hard enough to at least elicit what should have been a revelation to me.

"Dave," he said, with a thin smile, "let it be. When I go, I just want it to be a sad day for all concerned."

In retrospect, that said it all. In retrospect, I should have known: There was no will.

Tom was fed up with his three kids. Somewhere along the line, he decided that there was only so much that he could do for his sons—and he had already done it. Basically, Tom had written the kids off.

Or so he thought.

With no will, Tom had figured everything he had would go to Julie, as the surviving spouse; the kids would get nothing. Uh-huh. Welcome to America, the most litigious society the world has ever known.

People attend funerals for many reasons, most born out of their own loss or the desire to console the pain of others. But sometimes, they also attend to make sure the deceased is actually dead—because if he is, it's time to divvy up every asset he left behind. I don't know what is in the heart of any other person, and I don't want to ascribe motives to Tom's three sons who stood, wet-eyed, gazing into their father's casket. But in the days and weeks after the burial, it's entirely possible that what I saw were tears of joy. I base this on the fact that one son wandered over to me at the cemetery and introduced himself. As I started to offer condolences, he interrupted me.

"When's the reading of the will?" he asked.

And that brings us to the third thing you look for in estate planning: to make sure that the things go to the people you want to with the least possible expense and taxes incurred. This also did not happen, because within two days, the lawyers were involved.

Remember how Tom and Julie had split everything down the middle? This is where the problem started. Because there was no will, everything that was in Tom's name now was forced into probate. A court was going to decide who got how much of "Tom's" $1.2 million estate.

This happens more often than you might think. Interestingly, it is estimated that two-thirds of all the people in the U.S. die without a will. With the differences in state law, this can open a king-sized can of legal worms; it can become a grab bag for anybody who can gin up a plausible claim. And Tom and Julie's boys knew it. They banded together against their mother. They hired their own attorney to fight for a share of the estate.

Naturally, when I sat down with Julie, she was in tears over the situation. She could not believe it: First, she loses her husband, then her children turn against her.

"Despite everything," she said, "I thought we were a family." Her voice hardened. "I was wrong."

Fortunately for Julie, she had some assets in her name, so she could afford to pay the bills. Good thing, too—because when her kids went to probate court, the judge froze all of "Tom's" assets. I referred Julie to an attorney I knew to be experienced in probate and inheritance law. He cautioned her to prepare for months of litigation.

The bottom line? After eight months and tens of thousands of dollars in legal fees, the court finally came to the decision. Of the approximately $1.2 million that Tom had in his name, Julie was awarded $600,000; each of the three children received one-third of the balance—after some estate taxes that were paid.

"I was glad it was over," Julie later said to me. "I can

only hope that day is the low point in my life. I couldn't stand anything worse. My children—and they became so *predatory.*"

She had lost her husband and life partner. Now she had lost something more: a mother's trust in the love of her children.

Only time could heal those emotional wounds; however, financially we could get started right away. One of the problems in the probate case of Tom's estate was finding records of where things were, who owned what; Julie needed to find and organize the deeds, the titles—all the documentation of her asset base.

One of the first assignments for Julie: head for an office furniture store and buy a fireproof file cabinet with a good lock. I like these better than fireproof safes because they actually *are* file cabinets; you can organize the contents in the drawers, which are the standard size for file folders. As a practical bit of advice, put it down in your basement; it can weigh four hundred pounds or more. Then just cover it up with a tablecloth. If there is ever a burglary, it's unlikely the thief will even know it's down there.

Here's what you keep in it: financial statements, confirmation statements and retirement planning statements, anything with IRAs, Roth IRAs and/or other holdings of that nature. You'll want a file for insurance policies and another for your will or living trust; I'll talk about this in a moment.

In addition, create a file for tax returns. This will be a thick file, since I urge clients to keep ten years of tax returns. Even though except in cases involving fraud, the IRS requires you to keep them only three years, ten years is a pretty safe time frame. More file-folder content: marriage certificate, car titles, birth certificates, credit card statements, retirement plan beneficiaries, loans outstanding.

For Julie, things were simpler than they might be for you. Tom had operated on a "pay as you go" basis, so by the time he died, he had paid off the big-ticket mortgage and auto debts that burden most of us.

All this was a lot of work, but at least it would help Julie get going. It took her three weeks to handle this initial project, but when she was next in my office she was eager for more.

In the interim, a review of the documents Julie had compiled for the probate hearing had helped me to establish her current total net worth: about $1.8 million. Julie now had a decision to make. Under current tax law, she could leave up to $1 million to anybody without incurring estate taxes. In 2006, the law will change, increasing this figure to $2 million (though only briefly; in their infinite wisdom, our lawmakers passed a *new* law. If Julie dies in the year 2011 or later, the estate tax-free portion drops back down to $1 million).

But short term, we had a dilemma. Did we try to protect that extra $800,000 so as to avoid estate taxes, or did we simply hope that she would live another four years? After all, she was only sixty-five years old.

Let's say Julie opted for protecting it. How would we do it?

One of the simplest ways is through insurance. For example, we could buy a $300,000 life insurance policy on Julie; set up properly, in the event of her death, that $300,000 would go to somebody, *tax-free*. The heir would use this $300,000 to cover *all* the estate taxes owed on the extra $800,000 of taxable income in Julie's estate.

For some people, this would have been a great idea. But after what Julie had just gone through, she was a tad bitter. "I will not spend another dime to protect money for three ungrateful children," she told me.

I did not push the point; with her health and age, Julie was a good bet to live long enough to reach 2006, when the $2 million tax-free cap would go into effect. We could deal with the change set for 2011 at a later date.

With what we had in place, Julie and I now started on her estate planning. Remember step one? Any financial plan must start with the goal of providing enough money to live on for the rest of her life.

Because of her age and her resources, I recommended that roughly two-thirds of her money should be in conservative investments focused more on income than on growth; the remaining one-third of the investments could be targeted more aggressively. Julie had no problem accepting that ratio; she was comfortable knowing that not all of her eggs were in one basket, as long as we watched each basket closely.

To maintain her current lifestyle, Julie needed a pretax income of about $70,000 annually. The asset allocation easily provided at least that much, and in good years even more.

Unless something catastrophic happened, income-wise she was set for life—even when she reached the stage of life when she required more specialized assistance. I speak, of course, of nursing home care. Currently, nursing home care can cost from $40,000 to $60,000 annually, depending on where you live. Julie would have the money needed if and when the time came.

She would also have a substantial estate. And, knowing how she felt about what Tom had left for her to deal with, I felt comfortable raising the topic at this meeting.

"Tom left you with a mess to sort out," I said. "Regardless of how angry you are now, don't do the same thing when it's your time. You need to decide what you want to do with your assets when you go."

Julie nodded. After a moment, she said, "Say I want to put some conditions on whoever inherits my money. What can I do to make sure they have to follow my wishes, exactly as I state them?"

I'm always good for a few suggestions in this area, but I'm no attorney. We called in an estate tax attorney to talk with Julie in my office. Why call in a specialist? If you were going to have heart surgery, you would not hire a foot doctor; the same principle applies here. And while we're at it, here's a tip about hiring an attorney: Do not hire one just because you know him, or because she is a member of your church, or because your kids went to school with him. Instead, hire a professional who specializes in estate tax planning. The bar association can give you a list; talk to at least three. You want somebody who knows the ins and outs, the current laws, and who can have the answers to your questions. Don't settle for less than the best; it's worth the money. And make sure your personalities match.

How much money? In most parts of the country, expect to pay between $1,000 and $2,000 for your living trust; it may be a little bit more if you live in an area with a high cost of living. The size of the estate should not impact the cost appreciably, certainly not as much as the complexity of the trust document itself.

Why have a living trust instead of a will?

Simply, a will does not go into effect until your death. Most living trusts also have a will already incorporated into them. For that reason, a living trust is a document that can help you while you are living *and* after you die. For example, it can specify your wishes in case you have a disability or are unable to manage your affairs. Certainly, it helps you avoid probate at the time of your death. And finally, under certain circumstances and depending on the size of the estate, a living trust can also minimize the estate tax liability.

For all of the above (and other considerations that we'll examine in a moment), there are many good reasons to set up a living trust—and virtually no reasons not to.

Almost always, you want what is called a "revocable living trust." This means that if the tax laws change or a better option comes along, you can change the provisions. There are also irrevocable trusts which cannot be revised. For a few people, there may be reasons to opt for one of these, but those circumstances are relatively rare. The vast majority of people reading this book neither want nor need an unchangeable trust.

Because of the growing popularity of living trusts, there are a few points to consider when preparing one:

- **Do not buy a living trust or a document over the phone.** These are often fill-in-the-blanks generic forms that aren't worth the money. In addition, the risk of being scammed is simply too high.

- **Never buy a living trust from one of the seminars that you see advertised in the newspapers, magazines, or in the electronic media.** Almost always, you'll pay more and get less for it. Generally, what you will find in many of these "seminar" trusts is filler pages: The trust document may be a hundred pages long, but all the relevant information is on fewer than twenty. The rest is there to fool you into thinking you're getting more for your money. Often, it's all wrapped up in a neat leather binder to make it look even more impressive. Go to these seminars if you must; pick up an idea or two. Just beware of buying your trust document from these people.

- **Fund the living trust.** A living trust is just a document. Unless you do something called "funding the trust," that trust document is absolutely worthless. This means that you must take your assets—the title of your home, your car, your secondary property, any accounts you may have at the bank or brokerage house—and put them in the name of that trust. Occasionally, prospective clients come in with unfunded trusts. They had the trust document drawn up, and they think everything is in order, but the lawyer never explained what had to be done.

- **Name a trustee. Better still, name several.** All living trusts will have a trustee. Most people name themselves the trustee of the trust. So it might be the (your name) living trust, dated February 14, 2003, specifying (your name) as trustee. You are the only one who *controls* the trust; you also are the *beneficiary* of the trust. This means that in the name of the trust, you can invest, make purchases, sell property, withdraw money, and so on. But it's also a good idea to name what is called a "successor trustee." This is the person who will take over for you in the event that you cannot handle your own affairs because of incapacitation, whether temporary or permanent, or even death. In most cases, naming a successor trustee is not a problem. Most commonly, people name their spouse as their successor trustee. An adult child can be the successor trustee; if you have more than one child, you can either name one of them, a few of them, or all of them—or none of them, as Julie opted to do.

Sometimes, as a last resort, people will appoint a bank or a savings institution their trustee. But if you make the bank the trustee, you should stipulate that the financial advisor you use will continue to manage the fund. After all, he should know your goals and desires better than a bank.

Whoever you name as successor trustee, make sure they are savvy about exactly what you want. The trustee should know how to run financial affairs or at least know who to turn to in case of a problem. You must trust your trustee implicitly. Remember: You are giving him or her the rights to handle your affairs in the event of your incapacitation. During that time, while you're physically or mentally helpless, they can do just about anything they want with your estate.

Julie named her brother as successor trustee and her sister as the next successor trustee. When you are thinking about successor trustees, it's a good idea to name three or four, or even five of them; you never know what is going to happen down the road. Your first choice may pass on the honor, for whatever reason; if that happens, you want to have your affairs go straight to the next trustee in line. It's also a good idea to provide for payment of a stipend; you're asking a lot from your trustee, so it's only fair to compensate him or her.

And while we were discussing bequests, we also talked about the various worthy charities that exist. Julie could leave money to the Humane Society, the American Cancer Society, her church. She could endow a scholarship at the university she attended. Every year $5,000 or $10,000 could provide for a deserving student or help build a new wing on the library.

You can also maintain control of your own destiny, at least to a point. Another very valuable point of a living trust—one that should be included in *all* living trusts—is something called a living will. Many of you may have heard this term. It's received a lot of coverage in the media, particularly in this day of organ donation, transplants, and life-support systems that can prolong physical functions indefinitely. But it is pretty likely that most people don't quite understand exactly what it can and cannot do for them.

Remember how I said that it was very lucky for Julie that Tom died after only five days in intensive care? It sounds harsh to say it, but it kept Julie from having to make the emotionally devastating decision of whether or not to cease life support for her husband. And from a financial standpoint, it may have kept Julie from bankruptcy not far down the road.

Remember, Tom did not even have a "normal" will, let alone a living trust or a living will. Most courts in this country are very reluctant to pull the plug on somebody in a hospital, even in so-called "hopeless" cases. With intensive care unit costs that can reach several thousand dollars per day, it doesn't take a financial genius to see what this can mean. Ditto, if Tom had the ill luck to "survive" the stroke, only to require permanent nursing home or skilled medical care.

It's bad enough when that happens to a loved one. But what if it happens to you? With a living will, *you* make the choice—by yourself, for yourself.

What were the other advantages to Julie of setting up a living trust at this time?

The first question I asked Julie was who was it that we are really trying to protect, when she finally passed on. The answer surprised me, but I probably should have guessed.

Julie sighed, and rolled her eyes. "The kids, I suppose. They don't deserve it, but . . . well, they *are* my children."

A mother's love; it's one of the few constants in our troubled world, and thank heaven it is.

Because Julie was unfamiliar with estate planning, I provided her a little advice—just kind of thinking out loud, considering different alternatives. Fact: Julie could logically expect to have an estate of perhaps $1.8 million or more, after estate taxes and expenses.

Option one: simply divide this money into thirds, which would leave approximately $600,000 to each of her three sons, minus any estate tax liability. It's how they do it in the movies: split everything equally and let everybody go their separate ways. But because of the drug, alcohol, marital, and sundry other personal problems Julie's sons experienced, it might not be the best real-world solution.

What I suggested was this: Julie would set up three different trusts, one for each of her three children. Each would contain approximately 20 percent of the total value of her estate, after expenses and any taxes; under the provisions Julie would stipulate, only the interest would be available to each of the heirs.

"If you want," I told Julie, "your trust document could allow access to the principal after a certain period of time— maybe ten or fifteen years, longer, if you'd like. Or, after your death, we could automatically give them twenty-five percent of the principal every five years."

This approach would ensure that the children would benefit from their inheritance, but not be able to lose it all in a fit of poor judgment. It might be a major disappointment for them, especially if they were expecting an immediate windfall. But this time, it would also reflect Julie's judgment and wishes.

We even took this process one step farther. Julie had six grandchildren, so she could include a bequest that spread 30 percent of her estate evenly among those grandchildren— a trust fund that would help pay for a college education, for example, or the down payment on a first home. The final 10 percent of the estate would be distributed among her favorite charities and her alma mater.

"After all," I said, "there's no reason why all your money has to go just to your three sons."

Julie pondered for a moment; then a thin smile not unlike the one I remembered seeing on Tom's face a few years before came to her lips.

"I like it," she said. "I like this idea *very* much."

"I thought you might," I grinned.

A living trust can send a definite message, even from beyond the grave.

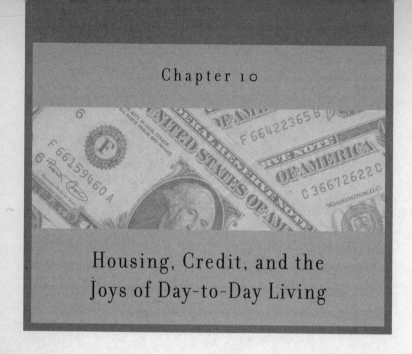

Chapter 10

Housing, Credit, and the Joys of Day-to-Day Living

In this chapter, we're going to do something difficult: We're going to look at a lot of different topics, all under the heading of "day-to-day living." We'll review housing issues, the agonies of buying a car, the need for (and problems of) establishing credit, and more. We'll even look at some of the frauds and scams that lie in wait for you out there.

And we'll do this in a series of stories—some short, some a little longer—on the various aspects of day-to-day living as a widow. Feel free to skip around if you wish, but there's a lot to be learned for everybody here.

Keeping House (Or Not . . .)

Here I am, a widow. I have a house, and I also have a question.

Now what do I do?

Again, remember Point 1 of our five-point program. You do nothing, for at least three months.

Well, not quite nothing: You can *think* about what you really want. You can even look around, to see what other options for you are out there. Perhaps you've already started this; perhaps before your husband died, you already were thinking about selling the place. You may already have a new place in mind.

Fine. But still take the ninety days. The house where you lived with your spouse for so many years may not be the same house without him, and I mean that for better *or* for worse. You need to use the time to find out.

And there may well be a lot of people pressing you to make an immediate decision. Some you need to take more seriously than others. For instance, if you can't afford the mortgage payments, that's a weightier matter than if a real estate agent calls with a really good condo listing.

And then there's the family. With a house, the kids really tend to stick their noses into the discussion. It is kind of like, "Mom, you do not need the house. What do you want with all that room, anyway? Let us move you to a condo, or a residential center for seniors." Or conversely: "Mom, you *can't* sell our house! I grew up here!"

Be strong. Of course, they have your best interests at heart, but another part of it may be . . . well, a little selfish, too. If it's so important for you to stay, are they willing to cut the grass, paint the porch, and handle all the other tasks involved?

Most often, it's the other way around. Especially if they live locally, the children have already considered the possibility that Mom may expect handyman help from the youngest kid, who is now forty-seven years old and probably has a house of his or her own. Coming over to cut the grass, clean the gutters, shovel snow, and all the other joys of home maintenance—well, suffice it to say that the novelty of it all has already worn thin.

In fact, it's pretty understandable. Do *you* want to deal with these chores? Probably not. It's one of the first reasons a widow gives for considering a home sale. She simply does not want to take care of the yard and house maintenance.

And that is absolutely wrong, because you'll be paying for it one way or another. Remember, if you go into a condo or to a town house, you will pay a property maintenance fee. It can range upward from $100 a month to basically pay somebody to come out and cut the grass, trim the bushes, shovel the snow—all the things neither you nor your kids want to do, but which are necessary wherever you choose to live. If you live in a major city, part of the fees you pay will go toward a doorman to help keep your building secure.

So if you *really* love your house, you can do what a condo association does: Just hire an outside maintenance firm that will give you a contract that says, "Okay, we are going to charge you x amount of dollars each month to cut grass, trim bushes, shovel snow." You can tailor the services to your inclinations (okay, maybe you *enjoy* using that Weed Wacker) as well as to your budget.

The point is, do not decide to sell your house simply because these chores have to be done and your late husband isn't around to do them. Certainly, don't sell because your children are too grown-up to cut grass anymore. Hiring your own person has advantages, too: If you are not satisfied with him, you can always fire him and get somebody else the next year. In a condo association or a family, firing people can get sticky.

So now we're forced to consider the real reason for or against selling the house. There are memories involved. Your spouse was there. Maybe your kids grew up under that roof. Answers to emotional questions usually take longer than those based on so-called "practicalities." Unless there is a real financial pinch—for instance, without the pension your late husband received, you just cannot afford to pay the taxes—playing a waiting game usually makes the best sense.

So just see what happens. You may want to keep the house longer because you still have grandchildren growing up. You like the idea of having them visit. You have more room and things like that. Conversely, maybe you want to travel and see the kids on their own turf.

Generally speaking, most widows do move out of the house sooner or later. Many times, I've found that the wife was ready to move to a condo or a smaller home many years before her husband died. He did not want to go because he had the woodworking shop in the basement. Sometimes it is a necessity: Your neighborhood could be deteriorating, and safety has become a factor.

Be that as it may, there is one other major mistake to avoid. Do not move merely to chase your kids around the country. Many sons and daughters will offer what sounds, at first, like good advice: "Why don't you sell the house and come out and live by me?"

Seldom does it work out, particularly in this age of casual mobility. You move out to California from Chicago, let's say—and all of a sudden your eldest son gets transferred to Dallas. *Now* what do you do? Pick up and move again? And again?

Some children will say, "Come on and move in with me." Generally speaking, this is an invitation to a disaster. As we all get older, we get set in our ways; that goes for us *and* our children.

Doing nothing for three months is also good advice in another part of the sell/don't sell equation. One of the things I see often is that widows love to redo houses when the spouse is gone, and they can easily go overboard. New bathrooms, new kitchens, new windows, new roofs—all the things the husband never did (or refused to spend money on) suddenly become high-priority items.

Marilyn, a friend and one of my long-term clients, did exactly this. She ended up spending much more money than the house was worth, given its location and overall age. In retrospect, Marilyn admitted, rather sheepishly, she would have been better off just selling and moving to a residence that was already new.

"From a financial standpoint, I mean," she corrected herself. "But doing all that was a kind of therapy for me, I think. It let me feel that I had a measure of control. It also let me ease into being in charge of my own life. I had to deal with all these people—roofers, contractors, plumbers. Doing all that renovation bought me time, and that's what I needed most at that point."

At the time, I was certain Marilyn had made the wrong decision. After all, when a man is widowed, he almost *never* does any of that stuff. But now I'm not so sure. Today, Marilyn lives in another place—a condo—in which she seems to be very happy.

"I moved," she told me recently, "when I was ready to go."

Buying Your Car: Marie and the Road to Perdition

Marie had been a client of mine for more than three years, and in many ways she was anything but the typical widow who sought out my help.

For one thing, it had been Marie who had handled virtually all the financial affairs of her family, even when her late husband Richard was alive. For another, she had seldom shown any hesitation at trusting her own judgment, even after one of the rare times it had led her astray.

Marie was smart and tough, and that was why I was so surprised to see her in my office, unannounced and without an appointment, one day in early April. But if the mere fact of her presence was a surprise, her first words astonished me.

"David, you have to *help* me," Marie said, her words coming in a rush. "I'm at my wit's end; I'm sure I've made a *terrible* mistake—" Her voice fell to an almost unintelligible mumble, and as I walked her over to a client chair, I could only discern the occasional word: "awful," "horrifying," and finally, "automobile."

"Good heavens, Marie," I said, waving urgently to my

staff to bring in refreshments. "What is it? Have you been in an auto accident?"

She shook her head, the expression on her face dismal and without hope.

"I think . . . I'm almost certain . . . that I just bought a new car."

It may sound humorous, unless it happens to you.

Marie had stumbled into one of the last vestiges of robber capitalism, the modern-day equivalent of cutthroat selling, the final frontier of highway banditry: the auto dealership.

Here's what happened to Marie. Like most people, the first thing she did was head straight for the cars on the lot or parked in the showroom. Marie wasn't alone for long; before she knew it, a salesperson (male, though an increasing number today are women) was at her elbow.

"He seemed very . . . *nice,*" Marie said, employing an adjective I had not heard this usually tough-minded woman employ in previous conversations. "And helpful. I mean, he even seemed to know all the kinds of things I wanted in a new car." Small wonder that, I thought.

A week or so before, Marie first began to think about trading up, and she had stopped briefly at another dealership across town. And by doing that, she had already put herself into play with the salesman she encountered today.

Before she had even closed her car door, he had typed Marie's auto license plate number into the dealership's computer. Because she had already stopped at another dealership that also was "on the system," he already had a basic credit/worth assessment on her. As he watched Marie walk toward the showroom entrance, he scanned the additional notes from the first salesperson with whom Marie had briefly talked.

He knew whether Marie still owed on her current vehicle, and what she paid per month on it, for instance; he knew what Marie said she wanted in trade-in value on her present car. He knew she had been looking at a midsized sports utility vehicle at the first dealership and seemed interested; that she intended to trade in her current car; that she had told the first salesperson that she liked "quiet" colors rather than the fire-engine red one that dealership had in its showroom.

He knew all this, just from what Marie had thought was a casual and anonymous conversation more than a week before. And he knew something more: Figuring she would not return to the first dealership anyway, Marie had spoken freely that day. Her new salesman even knew that Marie was a widow—and had never shopped alone for a car before.

Within an hour, Marie had been steered into a forest-green SUV ("The color just seems to suit you," the salesman told her); had been pressured into taking it for a test drive ("I have to photocopy your driver's license, just for insurance purposes" he said, and another treasure trove of data went into the dealership's computer); found herself "negotiating" (first with the friendly salesperson, then with a dizzying series of higher-ups, all of whom "her" salesman "fought with" to get Marie "the best deal possible"); and finally, almost before she realized it, went driving away in her new vehicle.

And that's when it all hit her, and she headed over to see me, distraught.

Welcome to the Free-fire Zone that is today's automotive marketplace. Today, both clicks (Internet auto shopping) and bricks (the traditional, showroom dealership) are using cutting-edge technology mixed with ages-old horse-trading tactics to target the car-buying public. It's a game that has long been stacked in favor of sharp-dealing experts, and the advent of the computer age has only lengthened the odds in their favor.

I will not make light of Marie's horrific experience; buying a new automobile is an experience that has daunted the brave and humbled the haughty since the days when the little old lady from Pasadena was still in pigtails.

It is an expedition into *terra incognito,* a trek off the boundaries of the known universe; it is an unfamiliar world populated with hostile natives and avaricious aliens who can strip the unwary to the bones in the blink of an eye—or the wink of one, since the perpetrator is almost always a pleasant sort of pirate. It is particularly hazardous to neophytes like Marie, who—despite her proven acumen in managing her life—still tend to equate "nice" with "honest."

Like many women, Marie assumed car bartering was a dark ritual of the male gender. Her first car came after college, a graduation present from her parents. It was the car traded in by the newlyweds on "their" first car as a couple. That time, as subsequently, Marie had always left the details of auto purchasing to her late husband, Richard.

Oh, she had sometimes accompanied him, Marie told me. She had watched while Richard had joked and scowled, kicked tires and slammed doors, nodded knowingly at engine blocks or smirked skeptically at the figures the salesperson would scrawl on a pad and pass to him.

"It all seemed rather . . . *silly,* " Marie confided. "As if it were some kind of tribal ceremony that'd you'd see on a *National Geographic* documentary."

Exactly. But the idea isn't to make car buying a men-only ritual; in fact, you'll never see a NO GIRLS ALLOWED sign on any dealership's door.

In fact, the end product of this intricate dodo dance is remarkably gender-neutral and entirely democratic in its objective. The goal is to help the auto dealer/salesman extract every possible penny of profit from every buyer. And don't be fooled: Almost every person (man or woman) who buys a car has been rough-vacuumed this way, to the tune of hundreds (and often, even *thousands*) of dollars.

I have a confession: I've always been somewhat interested in cars, in the same way that a teenaged boy is somewhat interested in girls. In my life thus far, I've owned more than one hundred and fifty automobiles. That's a lot of wheeling and dealing . . .

. . . and I'm still embarrassed by the mistakes I've made (and the extra money I've sometimes paid) for some of my automobile purchases.

But I've picked up a few tips along the way, which I volunteered to share with Marie. You might want to take notes, too.

First things first: The good news is that in the state where Marie had purchased her car, she was entitled by law to a forty-eight-hour reconsideration period. Even so, it took us the better part of the next day to extricate her from the agreements she had signed and to force the return of the deposit she had given the dealership.

Afterward, we went to work by starting back at the beginning.

Do You Need a New Car?

The question I asked Marie when she came in is the first question everyone considering a new car should ask first: What is wrong with your *current* car?

In Marie's case, she was driving a seven-year-old car with almost a hundred thousand miles on the odometer; she was starting to spend money regularly on repairs. As reasons go, this was a good one. You do not want to keep a car that has begun to nickel-and-dime you to death—and with today's typical repair bills, we're talking hundreds of dollars in nickels and dimes. It makes no sense when the repair bills start adding up on a car that is worth only a few thousand dollars; pretty soon, you've put much more money into it than you can recoup in resale value or even personal use.

Car Leasing: Don't. (But If You Do . . .)

There's one bit of advice I like to give people when they ask about car leasing.

Don't do it.

Oh, I know all the arguments: You get more car for the money, you avoid a lot of the hassles of maintenance and upkeep, you don't have to worry about the headaches of outright ownership, blah, blah, blah . . .

Don't do it.

For those true novices out there that do not understand leasing at all, think of it more or less like renting a car; basically, the title never transfers into your name but instead stays with the manufacturer.

Let's say you really like a car that has a sticker price (the manufacturer's suggested retail price, or MSRP) of $40,000. If you lease the car for thirty-six months, you can calculate the so-called residual value (that is, the value that car is going to be worth three years down the road) is, say, $20,000. That comes to a 50-percent residual, which is pretty common.

So what you do is take the $20,000 that the car is going to lose in value, divide that by the thirty-six months—and right there you have $555 a month. Roughly, that is what you are going to pay for that car—except that just covers the depreciation. So now you must add interest on that $40,000 for the duration of the lease. Depending on interest rates and any incentives from the dealer, this could add another couple hundred dollars to your payment, bringing it up to perhaps around $750 a month.

Now, leasing may be good for you if you prefer not to lock a lot of cash in the car. For instance, you may be earning a great return on your investments and don't want to take a big chunk of capital from them to buy a car.

Or you may like the idea of smaller payments: If you simply bought that $40,000 car and made payments on it for the next thirty-six months, your monthly payments would be substantially higher than $750. Or your accountant may advise you that a lease is the way to go because, in your particular situation, it allows you to save on taxes.

On rare occasions, you may have made up your mind that the $40,000 Gypsum SLT (a fictional name; who wants to be sued?) is the car of your dreams. Unfortunately, other potential car buyers don't agree, so sales have been slow for this model. So this may be one of the few times you're actually better off leasing than buying a car. If, for instance, the slow sales have convinced the manufacturer to offer a reduced rate of $499 for a three-year lease (in lieu of a cash rebate to help push Gypsum's sales, since that wasn't working anyway), it might be worthwhile for you. Rebates and deals come about for a simple reason: There are too many unsold cars sitting in lots and costing dealers (and manufacturers) money. Know this, and use it.

In all such cases, leasing may be an answer. Almost certainly, you'll be able to lease a more expensive car than you would get for the same money in purchase payments.

Still, at the end of the lease period, there is a major difference: If you're purchasing, you are actually going to own that car after, say, three years. With the lease, you own nothing but memories.

I still don't recommend leasing in most cases. But if you have good reasons to (or simply want to drive that bigger machine), at least consider what kind of lease is right for you.

LEASES: A PRIMER

Car leases are either *closed-end* or *open-end*. The difference is very important.

On a closed-end lease, you sign on the dotted line for payments of $750 a month. At the end of your thirty-six months, you simply walk away from the car. There is no further financial commitment, no concerns over residual value or anything else.

Not so with an open-end lease. An open-end lease is just what it sounds like. At the end of the lease period, the "owner" will sell the car; if it is worth more than what the lease terms anticipated, you will get money back. Conversely, if it is worth less than anticipated, you will have to come up with more money.

Usually, I never, ever recommend an open-end lease; there are too many variables involved. For example, that big battleship of an SUV that you loved so much? It gets ten miles to a gallon. What happens if gas is at $3.50 a gallon the day your open-end lease runs out? Nobody wants the gas-guzzling elephant, so the value of your vehicle goes down substantially. Most people just shouldn't take this risk.

But whether you have the closed-end lease or the open-end lease, always hanging out there is the Catch-22 of leasing: excessive wear and tear. "Excessive wear and tear" means different things to different people. A scratch on the fender that would not bother you may mean a substantial repair bill that you will have to pay when you turn that car in.

It can be very difficult to get a written definition of "excessive wear and tear" when you lease the car in the first place; it's even more difficult when you turn it in. Maybe you moved. Maybe the dealership changed hands. Verbal agreements that you thought you had suddenly no longer exist. When you return the vehicle at the end of thirty-six months, the dealer hands you a bill for $1,400 worth of reconditioning—for a car you thought was in fine shape.

How many miles do you put on a car? If you drive a lot, leasing quickly loses any cost advantage. Every lease out there is pegged to a specific mileage limit. More and more, in part to bring the price of the lease down to an attractive level, that mileage limit is being cut significantly back from what was offered in prior years. Today, most of the quotes you see advertised are for 10,000 miles per year. With the "average" driver logging 15,000 annually, the per-mile charge you incur can add up to serious money.

If there is *any* chance that you will not keep that car through the full lease term, do not lease. Penalties are very, very stiff if you need to get out of a lease early. Often, early termination could cost you thousands of dollars; increasingly, you'll be held to the strict terms of your lease.

Finally, I strongly recommend not to take a lease out longer than the warranty period on the car. Today, most cars are covered by a three-year, 36,000-mile warranty; if anything major happens to the car during this time, the manufacturer will fix it for those terms of the contract. (Beware: Accidents or abuse are a different story; you're liable.)

The problem comes when somebody takes out a four-year, or a forty-eight-month, lease on a car that has only a three-year warranty. Guess who must pay to fix anything that goes wrong after thirty-six months? You, of course. And who wants to pay to repair someone else's property?

There are other potential problems with leasing. For instance, many states differ in how they deal with sales taxes on leases versus buying. In Illinois, when you buy that $40,000 car, you will pay the roughly 7.5 percent tax *on the entire $40,000 "purchase,"* even though you are not actually buying the car. That's almost $3,000 just in sales tax. Other states run things differently, so it pays to investigate first.

By the way, I leased a car once, long ago. I was applying for a loan to buy an attractive property, and the bank was calculating whether I would qualify for the loan. Imagine my surprise when the bank factored in the remaining payments that I had left on the lease *as a liability*. It actually became a debit. In contrast, if I had owned the car, it would have been listed as an asset.

Another important factor is something called "gap insurance." Often it is included in the lease, but heaven help you if it's not and you need it.

Say you lease that $40,000 car and someone steals it later that day. As with all autos, the instant it left the showroom floor it lost thousands of dollars in value. You have made only that first payment of, let us say, $500. Your insurance company will insist it is not a "new" car and refuse to pay $40,000 in settlement.

Somebody has got to make up the difference on that loss; without gap insurance, that somebody is *you*.

There are other pitfalls to watch for, too. For instance, lease companies frequently make you agree to an "acquisition fee." This adds perhaps $300 or $400 in charges to you, essentially just to handle the paperwork for setting up the lease. In the same greedy vein, there can be "drop-off fees" when you return the car. Again, this can be $300 or $400; what you get is a bored clerk's initials indicating he has looked at the car. Sometimes these charges are negotiable, sometimes they are not—and that brings me to my last big point.

If you must lease, negotiate the deal. For some reason, people accept negotiating when they buy a car. With a lease, they mistakenly believe it is a fixed-price, nonnegotiable situation. Nothing could be further from the truth. The same rules apply to leasing as to buying.

This starts with doing your homework. Remember: If you are leasing a $40,000 car, the dealer actually pays perhaps $35,000 for it. Every thousand bucks that you get him to come down closer to that $35,000 figure equates to a smaller payment from you—in our example, about $30 a month for the life of that thirty-six-month lease.

Work for it, *fight* for it: After all, it is *your* money.

Buying a Car: Picking the "Ideal" Vehicle

That settled, I asked Marie what general type of car—sedan, pickup truck, luxury car, SUV, sports car—she wanted to buy. This is often seen as a personal preference only, but there are definite ramifications in other areas.

For instance, larger vehicles tend to be safer in an accident, but they tend to get lower mileage and when gasoline prices spike you'd better have the money to fuel this kind of gas guzzler. Marie could afford it, but can you?

Or: In a climate like Chicago, where I live, winter snow and ice make the four-wheel drive of an SUV very attractive. However, because SUVs ride higher than "normal" cars, some have been tagged with a reputation for rolling over too easily. And so on.

I also outlined to Marie the options that automakers offer on various models. Some of my favorite cars to look at for clients are those where pretty much everything comes standard. This is common on some foreign cars such as Hondas, Nissans, or Toyotas; many American cars take the opposite approach, offering a buffet of options that can pile thousands of dollars on top of the sticker price.

Know this about options: They can be very appealing, but three or four years from now when you sell the car, most likely you're going to get very, very little return for them. Most dealers focus on the condition of the trade-in and the total mileage. So buy the options you like, but understand that they will not give you much in resale value.

Now we were into the crux of the question. In order to determine a realistic price Marie would be willing to pay for a vehicle, we had to (1) decide on a specific make, model, and options; and (2) based on that information, determine the actual cost to the dealer of a vehicle so equipped.

Let the Games Commence . . .

Let's say that Marie decided she wanted an SUV—she did live in Chicago, remember—that (to avoid litigation) we'll call the Gas Guzzler 3000, made by a nonexistent Japanese company called Riceburner, Inc.

The Gas Guzzler comes with 4WD, air conditioning, CD player, sunroof, and leather seats standard, so we'll say there are no extra-charge options needed. And let's set an MSRP—manufacturer's suggested retail price, or what Riceburner, Inc. says the dealer *should* charge—at $30,000. But MSRP is the wish-list price: The dealer may want that much, but this is the never-never-land world of auto sales. He may try to charge much more at the same time he'd settle for significantly less.

Confusing? You bet; it's designed that way.

The "actual dealer cost" of any vehicle is the Holy Grail of prospective car buyers. As such, there's a lot of interest by dealerships (and auto manufacturers themselves) in keeping their vehicle cost confidential.

These days, there's a lot of arrogance among consumers. After all, you can log on to any number of Web sites and—presto!—you have the "Blue Book" or "Black Book" or Whatever-Color-Is-Fashionable Book valuation for any vehicle made, new or used.

It gets worse. Most people have heard of "invoice price," as in "I'll sell you this car at one hundred dollars over invoice price." The message is that the dealer makes only a $100 profit, which seems to most people only fair.

Well, it might be if it were true; it isn't. Invoice price is just one more scam to hook the clueless consumer. On a $30,000 vehicle, the "invoice price" he shows you will probably be no lower than $28,000, and may even be higher on popular, high-demand models—and even *that* is not the actual price the dealer paid to get the car into his showroom.

The "invoice" is padded, artificially inflating the so-called dealer cost. Why? To provide a built-in margin of profit, of course—sometimes only a few hundred dollars, sometimes significantly more. How? This built-in profit is called a "manufacturer's holdback," and it actually does go to the manufacturer. But only for a while, after which it is returned to the dealer. It's become an open secret in the industry, a wink-and-grin at the consumer's expense. Often, this holdback comes to 2 percent or 3 percent of the *retail* price—in this case it would be 2 percent or 3 percent of $30,000, or another $600 or $900.

What that means is that even if the dealer sold you that car "at invoice-plus"—that is, at $28,000 plus the $100—he is still going to get a check sometime during the year for another $600 or $900 on that car he sold you. While that check is signed by the manufacturer, in actuality it came from *you* in the hidden invoice overpayment you were charged.

In the case of the Gas Guzzler 3000, let's average the

two figures and call it a $750 holdback. The dealer's profit is now $850—the holdback, plus the $100 over invoice. Okay, now we're getting a little annoyed, but the guy's got to make a living, right?

Except we're not done yet. Add in those little items listed on most sales contracts, such as rustproofing/under-coating (actual cost about $100, but you are charged upward of $600), extended service agreement (dealer cost, between $100 and $500, for which you are charged about $1,500), an advertising fund charge, gas and oil . . .

. . . and, of course, the infamous "dealer prep" charges. By now, just about everybody has simply accepted dealer prep as a kind of inescapable welfare payment to the dealership. But beware: The amount can vary wildly. Sometimes the dealer even has two or more preprinted pads. One lists dealer prep for, say, under $100; the other could go several hundred dollars higher, and it is not unheard of for an unscrupulous dealer to switch pads after showing you the lower one. Check *every* time.

Have you been adding up the additional charges? In the case of the Gas Guzzler, these add up to almost $2,000, just in the charges we've listed. The dealer profit, if you sign on the bottom line, is now about *$2,800*—not bad for an hour's work, unless *you* happen to be paying it.

And remember that I said the *actual* price the dealer paid to get the car into his showroom most likely wasn't the "invoice" price; in fact, most likely it is as much as $2,000 lower—a couple of grand that goes straight to the dealership's profit column.

We're *still* not done yet. Are you trading in your old car?

Dancin' to the Oldies: The Trade-in Boogie

I always advise my clients not to tell the auto salesman a trade-in is involved *until a firm price has been set for the new purchase.* Why? The adage in the car business is: "It doesn't matter what pocket the money comes from, as long as it ends up in mine." Dickering over the trade-in allowance the dealer will "give" you is a time-honored method of fleecing the customer.

Stripped of all the smokescreen, the concept is simple. You pay for a new car by coming up with the agreed amount of cash (even if you finance, it's still cash money to the dealership), *minus the agreed-upon cash value of your trade-in.*

It's logical, really: What the dealer "loses" on one side, he makes up on the other. You may get what you consider a big discount on the new-car price, but it does you no good if you get snookered with a trade-in that is far below the *true* value of your old car (that is, what your trade-in is worth on the open market).

At every dealership, specialists are employed to quickly determine the condition and resale value of any car offered as a trade-in. Their job is to come up with a valuation that ensures that, when the dealer disposes of your car, he makes money on the deal—even if all he does is sell it at wholesale to another dealer or to an auto auction. The trade-in value he sets for your old car will be guaranteed to maximize dealer profit by minimizing the return to you.

This practice is called "lowballing," and it was ancient when Henry Ford was a schoolboy. But you don't have to accept the figures you're given—certainly not if they are far below what you've determined is your old car's actual worth.

The only way for you to know what your old car is worth is to *shop it around yourself.* Check all the books and Internet sites, of course; but also check the newspapers, supermarket bulletin boards, and even used-car lots to see how other cars of the same make, model, and year are being priced.

Ask to see a recent auction book for cars. In theory, this lists what dealers in your area have paid for the used cars they purchase at auction. In practice, you're always at risk when you count on documentation that is provided by people who count on your lack of accurate information to make their living. Ask for the auction book, but don't ignore your own need to research.

Financing the Deal

And if you've decided to finance, the games are not over yet. Every dealership can provide you with "convenient" financing, either through its manufacturer's credit division or through arrangements with local banks or financing companies. Inevitably, the dealership (or even the individual salesperson) receives a "gratuity" for steering you there. The result: more profit for the dealer (and significantly higher interest costs to you).

For example, say the bank quotes a financing rate of 7 percent to the dealership; the dealership will then turn to you and—in all seriousness—charge you 8.5 percent. The dealer pockets the 1.5-percent difference. This is one reason dealers absolutely hate cash deals; it eliminates one potential profit mechanism.

Shop for your own financing and eschew the "convenience" the dealership promises.

On-line Auto Sales, Buying Clubs, Services

As of this writing, GM is aligned with AOL; Ford has inked an arrangement with Yahoo! So what, you say? Okay, but information is power. Why else are you already being tracked virtually every time you visit an auto-related Web site? Today's marketing uses supercomputers to build profiles on current or prospective customers, and every little bit helps . . . them.

What makes all this ironic is that the so-called on-line buying and selling of vehicles is merely an extension of the dealership system. All "buying clubs" or "auto e-brokers"—everybody, in fact—must purchase through dealerships; vehicle manufacturers do not sell directly to these "services." In fact, it's the law: Every state has auto franchising laws that protect the dealership system.

The advantages of Web-based auto buying are, almost without exception, a myth. Don't fall for the hype; inevitably, you'll do better at a brick-and-mortar dealership if you can force yourself to negotiate, down and dirty.

The "One-Price" Option

For many people, the practices I've outlined above have frightened them so much that haggling over a car becomes a life crisis for them. This has led to the increase in popularity of so-called one-price operations, which advertise themselves as a customer-friendly alternative. The price for each car is firm, the sales staff is low-pressure. Everybody wins, right?

Not necessarily. One price means just that: Take it or leave it, and most often you'll pay more than you would if you effectively negotiated with a "traditional" auto dealership. Sure, you're no longer forced to play horse trader, but remember, you will pay for that privilege, sometimes substantially.

A point to remember: With a new car, it's always courting disaster to finance your purchase for an amount that is higher than the *actual, titled-vehicle* value. It's a staggering realization, but a new car can lose an average of *40 percent of value* the moment you drive it out of the dealer's lot. All too many loan institutions will finance a new-car purchase for more than that (much more, when you figure in the loaded up-front interest on the forty-eight- to seventy-two-month loans available).

The charming term bankers and dealerships use for a person in this situation is "in the bucket." I've also heard it called being "upside down." Either way, you're in an unenviable position.

In practice, it means that you not only have no equity in "your" car for much of the foreseeable future—you actually are stuck with a car that is worth *less* than what you owe on it. If you try to sell or trade it in—or, heaven forbid, ill fortune and financial problems result in a repossession—you both lose the car *and* still owe a prince's ransom on the unpaid balance.

One last warning on credit purchases of cars: The shorter the loan period, the better. This seems self-evident, but in the emotion of buying the showroom-fresh car of your dreams, common sense is easily forgotten. Car selling is largely letting you do what you want to do, and auto salespersons know this. They know you really want the top-of-the-line model; they know you want to believe that you can afford it, too.

The tool of choice is the monthly-payment scam. If you blanch when the salesman quotes you a monthly payment of $895, a little number-crunching can bring the figure down to $525. How? By turning the initial forty-eight-month-loan figure into the lower seventy-two-month-loan rate.

The only problem: Over the lifetime of the longer loan, you'll pay as much as *three times more,* due to the higher interest rate and longer time you'll be financing it.

I'm convinced that the expression caveat emptor—in English, "buyer beware"—was invented by a freshly fleeced owner of a new car.

Buying a car need not be the modern-day equivalent of being drawn and quartered (or, perhaps more aptly, being skinned alive). But it takes effort. You must do your homework, you must commit to shopping around, you must be prepared for an arduous and possibly contentious negotiating session.

Marie found her motivation to do exactly all that. She was livid when she examined the carefully planned campaign her auto dealer had used to close the sale. Rather than get mad, though, she got even.

She spent the better part of the next week studying many of the tactics I've outlined here and game planning her next trip to the auto dealership. She prearranged her financing (through her own bank) and sold her old car through an ad in the local newspaper.

Marie is driving a new car today, by the way. And she bought it all by herself.

I wave as she drives by, because I've never seen anybody smile any bigger.

The Holy Trinity: Three Rules of Car Buying

Rule 1: Remember, no matter how genial he or she seems, the salesperson is not your friend. You will *never* make him your friend. Don't let this worry you. You already have enough friends anyway, and a car dealership is no place to troll for any more. I'm certainly not advising you to be rude, and I don't want to come across as overly cynical. But keep in mind that no matter how "nice" he or she seems, you are one thing to this person: a commission check, pure and simple. Forget that only at your financial peril.

Rule 2: For most dealerships today, the car is only the start of the profit-making machine; even if you have done an outstanding job of negotiating to get the rock-bottom, absolute-best price on your new car, the dealership is banking on making back that money (and more) through lowballing your trade-in, through manipulating your financing, through the sale of options, etc.

You can shortstop this by simply not letting the game continue.

The ideal way is to do your homework first, then keep your cards hidden. It helps you fight fire with fire. Remember: This is your money. He is entitled to make a reasonable profit off of you. He is *not* entitled to make a killing off you.

Rule 3: Be prepared to walk away—*at any stage in the process!*

If something happens that you don't like, or don't understand, stand up and thank the salesman for his time. Be prepared to get in your car and drive away—then do it, if the tune doesn't change, quickly and radically.

This isn't a negotiating tactic (though it usually works wonders as one). Rather, it is the *Prime Axiom of Car Buying*.

Watching a promising prospect walk out the door is the greatest fear at any dealership, where the entire process is designed to keep you there until your money is in their pocket. They know that once you leave, the statistics say you won't be coming back—and a competing dealership is always a little way down the road.

That's the whole reason why any car shopper can expect to be "handled" by a long line of salespersons, sales managers, trade-in estimators, service-department managers, business managers, finance managers, *ad infinitum.* The theory is that as long as you are still there, they're still pitching; sooner or later, if only from sheer sensory overload, you'll buy *something . . .*

However, there are some buyers who simply can't make themselves walk away. They've done the test drive, smelled the fresh leather, stroked the contours of what they are already seeing as "their" new car. Walk out? Are you *crazy?* I'll lose the chance to own this beautiful—

Maybe. But even if this particular dealership lets you go, so what? Remember this about cars: They make them in factories. They are not unique works of art or one-of-a-kind opportunities that must be seized without delay. Thousands of these vehicles roll off the assembly lines every day, and each of them must be sold to somebody if the whole system is to continue to work.

This is your leverage. Use it well.

Credit Where Credit Is Due

By now, everything should be starting to come together for you.

You're learning to deal with the loss of your husband; you've told the kids to keep in touch but let them know that you are quite capable of running your own affairs; you have found a great new financial advisor who is helping you get back on track financially; and you're starting to enjoy a world that you never dreamed existed only months before.

Now what?

Perhaps you've decided it's time to reward yourself and purchase that shiny new automobile. Or maybe you've decided to stay in your old house. So why not get those new windows and carpeting and update the master bedroom bath? After all, it's what you've wanted to do for years.

So you're thumbing through a stack of home remodeling magazines when the telephone rings. You check the caller ID. Great! It's the car dealer you visited yesterday. He's probably calling to tell you when you can pick up the shiny new car you simply fell in love with, and—

Scre-e-e-e-e-e-e-ch . . . CRASH!

"What do you mean my credit is no good?"

Sad to say, this kind of news is not uncommon for many women who have lost their spouses. Most of them can't believe it, understandably.

"When Tony was alive," a widow I'll call Teresa told me recently, "we always paid our debts on time. There weren't all that many bills, either—Tony hated owing anybody, and he'd pay in cash for any major purchases. Even so, we'd always get those free credit cards in the mail; Tony would cut them into pieces and put them in the trash." Her voice rose, indignantly. "How *dare* anyone say I'm a bad risk?"

What Teresa discovered is the insanely illogical contradiction that powers the credit industry: When you don't need the money, everybody is falling over themselves to give it to you. But when you *do* need it, well . . . suffice it to say it becomes much tougher to get the credit at all. Banks, stores, credit card companies, et cetera—all of a sudden, they no longer know your name.

And I mean that literally, particularly when you are a widow. You have no credit history—*in your own name!*—and that means you are automatically considered a credit risk. Tony could have gotten the loan painlessly; Teresa's loan application gets bounced without a second thought.

It's very similar to trying to land that first job out of school. No one wants to hire you because you have no experience, but how do you get experience without a job?

If you've gone through life paying cash for everything, or this is your first loan on your own, you have never really shown your trustworthiness to repay a loan, which is what credit is all about in the first place. Whoever is extending you credit wants the assurance that you not only have the ability but also the intent to repay your loan.

Don't worry: If you're having problems getting credit, it can be remedied. Here are a few ways to establish your own credit in your own name.

Let's start with what your potential lender is going to be looking for. It all begins at that small table where you fill out the application for a loan; it may be in an auto dealership or a bank, or even a department store so you can buy that new refrigerator you want delivered this week. You sign on the dotted line, giving permission for the next step: a credit check provided by one or another credit bureau.

There are hundreds of these, but the majority of them are affiliated with one of three nationally known credit-reporting companies or their affiliates: TransUnion from Chicago, Illinois; Experian from Orange, California; or Equifax out of Atlanta, Georgia. The lending institution will then use the information it receives to make a decision on whether or not to extend you the credit you seek.

Trust me, credit-reporting companies have the power to make your life a living hell. Every day, millions of pieces of information about people just like you are flowing over data lines to supercomputers these companies employ to track hundreds of millions of individuals. Ever miss a payment, or even send it in late? It gets reported. Declare bankruptcy? It's in the data bank. Get divorced, serve prison time, change jobs—it's all part of your computerized financial profile.

Worse still, the information that gets compiled in your credit report file may not even be accurate.

With all this data zipping around, it's inevitable that mistakes will occur. A misread digit here, a slip of the keyboard there, a tiny fluctuation in the electrical current passing over a silicon chip and—bingo! The wrong data is suddenly a part of your file.

Big lesson here. You remember that burly guy on TV? The one who says "Check your blood sugar and check it often"?

The same principle applies to your credit report. By law, you are entitled to request a copy of your credit report once each year; you can do this by computer, mail, or even telephone (*see contact information on page 222.*)

Find a mistake? Report it in writing and insist that it be corrected *immediately.* It could save you a lot of embarrassment later, not to mention getting turned down for that all-important loan you need.

It's important to understand what any potential lender is looking for in your credit report. Essentially, this breaks into three main areas that the industry terms "the three C's"—that is, capacity, character, and collateral. These areas allow a simple yes-or-no answer to any credit or loan you request. Let's take a look at each of the C's.

Capacity

Simply stated, the creditor is looking for evidence of your ability to repay the loan you are requesting. This category gives the creditor an insight into how good a money manager you have been, so obviously they need to know all the basics.

For instance, they look closely at your income. How

much do you earn every month? Are you eligible for bonuses? Do you have a second job, or any other secure income coming in except your job (i.e., rental income, alimony, child support, and so on)?

Of course, the other side of this coin is just as important. How much do you spend each month? You may make $5,000 a month, but if you already spend $6,000, the lender knows you can't possibly repay him; you definitely won't get the loan. But you may also be bounced if you're spending only $4,000. Here's why: The tool a lender uses to determine this is called your "debt-to-income ratio." It's relatively simple to figure this ratio out for yourself. Add up all your monthly expenses (mortgage payment, auto loan, credit cards, etc.—and don't forget to include the monthly payment on the item you are trying to purchase). Now divide that amount by the *total monthly income* you receive. This will give you your debt ratio.

If that number is 40 or below, that's good; at or around 50, you're a borderline case; 60 or higher, and you'll probably get the "don't call us, we'll call you" story.

Character

Here the lender is looking at your stability and your past history of paying your bills promptly. Have you moved seven times in the last five years? Had three jobs, all in different fields since last Christmas? Ever had your car repossessed? Had an account charged off against you lately?

The lender will score all these things against you—in a *very* negative way.

If this is a pretty accurate picture of you, get a good

coat of wax on that old beater you drive. Most likely, you'll be driving it for at least another year or two. It will take that long for you to get your credit rating turned around.

Collateral

This one is simple; even old Scrooge in *A Christmas Carol* insisted upon it. Collateral is that property you pledge against the loan, the tangible item that guarantees the lender will get his money back should you fall on hard times.

For example, the car you purchase will have the automobile itself as collateral for your loan. Say that you don't make the payments. At some point, a man will come and take the car from you and sell it to get their money back.

But you can use anything of value for collateral—as long as it is liquid, meaning readily converted to cash. Stock certificates, bonds, CDs, and real estate are all examples of good collateral. A set of false teeth and your late spouse's hearing aid are not.

All three of the C's are important to a lender, but because so many people today fall into the gray areas, sometimes lenders have to weigh the situation. If it is too close for the computer to call, your application will probably be given to a real live loan officer who will approve or disqualify you. The loan officer's job—and a thankless one it can be—is to add the human dimension. He or she will look at all the conflicting information and give the final thumbs up or thumbs down.

Given all these factors, what is the primary action you

can take to improve your credit? It's a no-brainer: pay your bills on time and as scheduled.

I've heard it too many times: People boast about how they cheat the system, earning a couple of extra pennies by leaving their money in an interest-bearing account and sending their payments at the last minute. Penny-wise but pound-foolish. Sooner or later, this behavior will come back to haunt you.

But let's say that you have been turned down for a loan or credit card because of bad credit or no credit rating. I recommend that you take the following steps—and do so immediately, so that when you need credit again you will have it.

Start with Your Local Bank

Ask around until you find a bank that will report your activity monthly to one or all three of the big credit rating services. Keep searching until you find one or more that does.

Then open a small savings account—say, $2,500. Wait a few weeks after it is opened, then go back in and request a loan for $1,500 *using your savings account as collateral.* Most banks will gladly do this. Why not, since they have no risk? If you don't make the payments, they can just take the money right out of the account they are holding.

If you have extra money, repeat this process at several banks. Of course, you will lose control of the money in these accounts, since the banks will not let you withdraw money as long as you have loans against it. But remember: You are not doing this to make money; *you are doing it to establish credit.*

Don't Panic, and Don't Pay Cash

Many widows have the cash to pay for that new car, using savings or the life insurance payoff. The urge is to avoid the credit hassle entirely; the temptation is to simply write out a check.

Don't do it. This is a golden opportunity to build a good credit record.

Let's say the purchase price is $25,000. Put down $15,000 and borrow the rest for about nine months. This will give your sagging credit rating a significant boost. Make every payment on time during that nine-month period. Then, if you wish, go ahead and pay off the loan early. You'll look great in the eyes of the next lender. This is especially true with some of these low- or zero-percent financing deals manufacturers come up with occasionally.

I'm often amazed at the decisions people make about their finances. I always have a couple of clients who are visiting auto showrooms, looking for a shiny new car. But even when a zero-percent-financing promotion is under way, there will always be one or two who will take money out of their account to pay the car off in cash.

I try not to pull my hair from my scalp as I ask them why. Their only response: "I've never owed anybody anything in my life; I'm not about to start now." Okay, but they are giving away literally thousands of dollars in free interest over the life of the car. Ironically, these are often the same people that will drive all the way across town to save ten cents on a can of corn at the grocery store.

Go figure.

Build a New Credit History

So you don't have the money to open savings accounts all over town, and you can't afford the buy-a-car suggestion above. You can still take steps that will improve your credit standing.

For instance, find a large department store in your area. Stop in and tell them you are thinking of making a purchase—a sweater, books, curtains—anything you might normally purchase anyway for cash.

Ask the store if they report your activity on their store credit card monthly to any of the major credit reporting agencies I've previously mentioned in this chapter. If they do, request a credit card from the store, even if it has a limit of only a few hundred dollars. If they approve you (and many will), purchase your items with their card. Then make the payments, on time and in full. Duplicate this process at other stores, wherever possible.

Use a "Secured" Credit Card

Most people with good credit get an "unsecured" card; they pay nothing up-front for the card, and the company that issues it takes a chance that the cardholder will pay the bill each month.

If your credit is unsatisfactory, you probably don't

qualify for an unsecured credit card. But you can still get a credit card, and use it to build (or rebuild) your credit rating. You do this by obtaining a *secured* credit card through a major bank.

What is a *secured* credit card? In plain language, it is a credit card you get after putting up a monetary deposit—for instance, $500. This, or some percentage of this amount, becomes your credit limit on the card. Don't worry: When you use the secured Visa or MasterCard, no one can tell that it is a secured card, not even if they call in the transaction for approval. You send in your monthly payments just as you would with an unsecured credit card.

Of course, the bank holds your $500; if you don't pay your bill and it has to close the account, the bank simply seizes the amount due. You'll get plenty of notices from the collection agency before that happens.

But if you make your payments on time and don't get yourself into any other financial difficulties, after about two years, most banks will offer you an *unsecured* credit card or, at minimum, increase the credit limit of your card without requiring an additional deposit from you.

A word of caution about secured credit cards. *Only deal with legitimate major banks that issue these types of cards!* There are tons of unscrupulous people waiting to prey on people in need; this area is no exception. Visa and Master-Card deal only with banks that put the name of their institution on all sales literature. If you don't see a name you know, throw it out.

Always ask the bank for specific information on annual or application fees the bank will charge for the card, how much interest it will pay you on your deposit, the interest rate it will charge you on outstanding balances, the length of any grace period allowed between payments, and what percentage of your deposit becomes your credit limit (ideally, all of it). Shop around, sort through them all, and pick the one that offers you the best overall terms.

Ensure that the bank you choose does *not* report to the credit agencies that yours is a *secured* credit card. To a lender, a secured card says that you have bad or no credit and were forced to use this type of program just to get a credit card. Don't be embarrassed; ask, and keep searching for a bank that gives you what *you* need.

Try a Little Help from Your Friends

If all else fails, you need a co-signer. This is a friend or relative who will sign on the dotted line next to your name and essentially guarantee that if you don't repay the amount of the loan, he or she will. Legally, a co-signer is next in line to pay off the balance if you default.

It's likely that your co-signer will be put through the same financial scrutiny as you, including a detailed credit-history report. This only makes sense. What good does it do the lender to have two unqualified applicants sign for the loan instead of one? This is one case where there isn't necessarily safety in numbers.

Remember: Both you and your co-signer are on the hook. If you don't make payments as scheduled, you hurt your own credit *and* jeopardize the credit of your friend or relative. Be sensitive to this fact, and be responsible.

The Credit Report: (Or, There Really *Is* a Permanent Record . . .)

Your credit report is vitally important, but it's not always accurate. You must check it and check it often; I recommend doing this annually, just to be safe.

Obtain a copy of your personal credit report periodically. It's free when you've been denied credit and $10 or less in other situations. Vigorously dispute any misinformation you find; unchallenged, an error can remain in your credit file forever.

Equifax Credit Services
P.O. Box 740241
Atlanta, GA 30374
Toll-free: 1-800-685-1111
www. equifax.com

Experian
P.O. Box 2002
Allen, TX 75013
Toll-free: 1-888-397-3742
www.experian.com

Trans Union
P.O. Box 2000
Chester, PA 19022
Toll-free: 1-800-888-4213
www.transunion.com

"May I See Your Driver's License? It Will Just Take a Minute . . ."

These days, life can seem to become more complicated with each passing moment.

Remember when our friend Marie visited the auto dealership and, in all innocence, handed the salesman her driver's license "for insurance purposes"?

On a recent business trip, I was scanning through *The New York Times* when the following story* caught my eye:

BOSTON *(March 21, 2002)*—About 10,000 people a week go to The Rack, a bar in Boston favored by sports stars, including members of the New England Patriots. One by one, they hand over their driver's licenses to a doorman, who swipes them through a sleek black machine. If a license is valid and its holder is over 21, a red light blinks and the patron is waved through.

But most of the customers are not aware that it also pulls up the name, address, birthdate, and other personal details from a data strip on the back of the license. Even height, eye color, and sometimes Social Security number are registered.

"You swipe the license, and all of a sudden someone's whole life as we know it pops up in front of

* *Copyright © 2002 The New York Times Company. Reprinted by permission.*

you," said Paul Barclay, the bar's owner. "It's almost voyeuristic."

Big Brother lives.

The bar owner may have purchased the machine to jack-light the fake licenses often carried by underage drinkers. But the wealth of information he could obtain, just from the magnetic strip on a driver's license, was irresistible. Quickly, he began to build his own data base of personal information on his bar's customers, providing an intimate perspective on his clientele that can be useful in marketing. "It's not just an ID check," he said. "It's a tool."

With the machine, he can subdivide and list his clientele by sex, age, zip code, or other characteristics. As the *Times* article noted, "If he wanted to, he could find out how many blond women named Karen over 5 feet 2 inches came in over a weekend, or how many of his customers have the middle initial M. More practically, he can build mailing lists based on all that data—and keep track of who comes back."

More than 90 percent of people in the United States aged twenty-one and up are licensed to drive. Almost every state now issues licenses with either a magnetic strip or a bar code that allows access to personal data; the handful of states that don't already do so plan to adopt the system over the next few years.

That means most of us will be carrying our life stories in our purses or wallets, an open book to anyone with the easily obtainable technology to read them. When it comes to privacy, the odds are definitely turning against the average person.

Your Credit Card Numbers:
For Thieves, It's Now a Global Market

A friend of mine who is a Chicago-area novelist met me for lunch a few weeks ago. As writers do, we began talking about our current book projects; I mentioned that one of my chapters dealt with the various credit card frauds that were striking more and more people with every passing—

I stopped, surprised at the expression on his face.

"What's wrong?" I asked.

He reached into a briefcase and rummaged through it briefly. Then he handed me an envelope with a familiar blue-and-white logo on the corner. It bulged with what looked like an inch-thick sheaf of paper inside.

"That's my most recent credit card bill," my writer friend said. "There are charges from places like Algeria, Pakistan, the Bahaman Islands—and I haven't been out of the country in two years."

My friend had discovered, to his dismay, just how widespread credit card theft is in today's world.

And "world" is no understatement.

According to Matt Richtel, a reporter for *The New York Times,* tens of thousands of stolen credit card numbers are being offered for sale *each week* on the Internet. In his story published on May 13, 2002, Richtel pointed to a number of membership-only sales sites on the World Wide Web that are operated largely by residents of Eastern Europe and Asia (specifically, Malaysia) and—by far the most active—the former Soviet Union. Today, as the Russian *Mafiya,* the latter group has become the central force in credit card and identity theft.

And we're not talking about people picking your pocket and walking off with the plastic card therein; they do not need the card at all. All they need is the number on it, and they obtain it in a number of simple ways. The waiter at your favorite restaurant may make an "extra" imprint; the clerk at your favorite boutique may freelance as a card-number thief, zapping your numbers to Odessa or St. Petersburg or Moscow via e-mail every night.

Devious computer hackers can even obtain the card numbers by breaking into the computer systems of on-line merchants, thereby obtaining *thousands* of credit card records at a time.

There are any number of sources that feed your credit card number into the black market network—in total, to the tune of more than *$1 billion* each year.

Richtel's article noted just how brazen these criminals have become, describing how they use what he termed "cyberbazaars"—Internet sites or chatrooms—where dozens of these lowlifes regularly log in for an on-line auction of the stolen card numbers. There was even discussion of a proposed criminal gathering at a credit card reseller's conference in Odessa, Ukraine—a fun-and-frolic convention of arrogant international credit thieves.

"(Recently) . . . the cost of a single credit card has been between 40 cents and five dollars, depending on the level of authenticating information provided. But the credit card numbers typically are offered in bulk, costing, for example, $100 for 250 cards, to $1,000 for 5,000 cards, with the sellers offering guarantees that the credit card numbers are valid," he wrote.

"In the old days, people robbed stagecoaches and knocked off armored trucks," said one official of the Computer Security Institute, an association of computer security professionals. "Now they're knocking off (computer) servers."

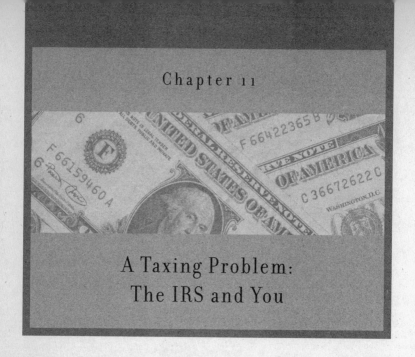

Chapter 11

A Taxing Problem:
The IRS and You

Mention the word *taxes* and the acronym *IRS* in the same sentence and watch the faces in your audience suddenly pale. In practice, any discussion of the United States taxation system—at least, as it relates to the citizens who, the IRS insists, "voluntarily" cooperate in the program—is more than enough to terrorize most mortal beings. In addition, we all grew up hearing the black-humor jokes our parents told about death and taxes.

By the time we reached adulthood, we knew better: They weren't jokes—they were all true.

As a nation, the United States first waded into the morass of a federal income tax in 1862. The idea—to fund the staggering cost of the Civil War—proved unpopular with the people and was dismantled ten years later. Like the rest of the fearful undead, however, the income tax would not remain buried. It rose again, rearing its frightful visage in 1913, once more with the specter of war as the professed reason. This time, it remained as a permanent feature of federal governance.

More time has probably been wasted in Congress and on campaign trails throughout this great country talking about taxes than about any other topic. If politicians aren't talking about how and who to tax, then the debate centers on how and where to misspend the taxes they do collect.

Each year, more than 200 million tax returns are filed in the United States. By this means, more than $1 trillion is collected by over 100,000 employees of the Internal Revenue Service, itself empowered by an almost $7-billion budget. This includes personal, corporate, estate, gift, and other types of returns. Ever wonder how much is $1 trillion? One could spend $1,000 a second, *every second,* for the next thirty-plus years—and still have money left over. That's $1 trillion, and this tax total doesn't even include the state, local, property, and sales taxes collected each year.

You've probably heard of Tax Freedom Day. This is an unofficial milestone that marks the workday on which the U.S. population has "earned out" our collective tax bill; it's when we actually start putting money in our *own* pockets. The actual date changes annually, depending on the various tax brackets—but in general Tax Freedom Day arrives somewhere around May 15 each year. That means *all the money you make up until May 15* goes into various government coffers.

I do not intend this to be a section on how to do your own taxes, but instead I want to take some time to reflect on some ideas on taxes themselves. Years ago, wearied of trying to work through the intricacies of the Tax Code alone, I joined the ranks of those who have turned their annual obligation into a spectator sport: I take all the numbers to my CPA, a proven specialist in this dark art.

Should you do likewise?

Believe it or not, some people enjoy doing their own taxes. If you are one of these, read no further; your decision has already been made.

As for everybody else (and I'm confident we're in the majority), as with most decisions in life, this one comes down to a matter of money. If you have the funds to pay the fee, I strongly urge that you use a CPA. This cost can run from $100 (the low side, usually for a very simple return) to several thousand dollars (and if you're at this level, you probably need an expert accountant in any event).

I seldom recommend any of the large national tax-preparation chains to my clients. With these, you never know what level of experience (or even competence) you will get when you walk in. Some of these preparers are very good indeed, but others are part-timers or one-shot wonders you may never see again (or want to).

It's almost always better to look for the tax preparer who has his or her own name on the shingle. You have a far better chance that this person will be there for you—all year long, year after year.

Even if cost is a consideration, I still urge my clients to consider using a CPA. This is particularly true when they have multiple income sources, various long- and short-term capital gains to report, limited partnerships, two or three brokerage accounts, and any other complexity in their financial life. The more complicated the return, the more you will need their help. And it usually pays off. A good CPA likely can save you taxes in areas that you would never have conceived of on your own. After all, that's how he justifies his fee.

To find a good one, ask around among your friends who they use, and why (or if) they'd recommend their accountant to you. Make a list, then do your homework. Compare prices; don't be afraid to ask for a discount or to counteroffer a lower fee. The worst thing they can say is no, and in that event you move to the next name on your list.

But if you still think you would like to go it alone—do it. Even with a complicated return, if you're relatively competent on a home computer, you can buy one of the nationally sold tax return programs. One of my favorites is Turbo Tax, but in the months before tax time the major computer magazines all review the different programs on the market. These programs have gotten good; each will walk you through every step of your return and prompt you on what to do. Another advantage: All the forms you need to file your federal (and often, state) tax returns are incorporated into the program. When you're done, the computer prints out only the forms you need, filled out, and ready to be mailed.

But if computers are not your cup of tea, you can always resort to the traditional method: the familiar do-it-yourself forms and packets issued by the IRS. You can request these from the IRS (on-line at www.irs.gov), but the full range is also usually found in local post offices and libraries. All you have to do is sharpen a #2 pencil and get to work.

No system is completely audit-proof, of course, but

here are ten guidelines that should help reduce your chances of joining the 2 percent or so of all returns that are audited each year.

1. Check your math; trust me, the IRS definitely will. You don't want to give them yet another reason to hold up your return for additional scrutiny.

2. Report *all* income. In today's computerized world, the IRS receives billions of records each year on income paid to you and every other taxpayer in the country. They almost always know about it already; report it the first time, and you won't have to explain it during an audit.

3. Answer every question. Despite its reputation, the IRS cannot read your mind. (At least, not yet.) Even if a particular line or question does not apply to you, don't leave it blank—write in "N/A" ("not applicable"). This way they do not have a reason to contact you (and possibly open up a can of worms on an unrelated issue).

4. Be neat and organized. Neatness *does* count. If the IRS has to guess whether your *2* is a *7,* it becomes just as easy to look at everything else on your return.

5. Use the right forms. The IRS expects you to put the correct information on the correct form. Fail to do this, and you become a problem for its staff to resolve.

6. Make sure all your numbers match. If you are submitting W-2, mortgage deductions, 1099s, and so on, make sure all your numbers match the reported statement numbers that the IRS gets from employers, banks, and others. If they don't match, get the numbers straightened out *before* you file your return.

7.   Never "round off" numbers unless they were reported that way on a statement submitted to the IRS. The IRS simply doesn't believe in coincidence. Get too sloppy with approximate numbers and they will come knocking.

8.   Here's an adage for all taxpayers: When in doubt, take all the *gray* areas, but none of the *black* ones. That is to say, as long as you can support any position you take on your tax forms, fine. The IRS code is so complicated you could ask three different IRS agents the same question and get three different answers. However, make sure your position is solid, not something akin to "I don't think that tax is fair and I'm not going to pay it." They are interested in IRS code, not your personal opinion.

9.   File your return on April 15. At least in theory, by filing as late as possible in the year, the IRS has less time and opportunity to audit your account. Presumably, the IRS has already flagged most of the accounts it will audit for that year. While the IRS has never admitted this is true, I think it's worth considering. Some people even file for an extension, just to take it one step further. But remember, if you do file for an extension, you must pay at least 90 percent of the tax you will owe to the IRS by April 15.

10.   Don't forget to sign your return. This simple (and common) mistake can cause adverse consequences—if only because it puts a spotlight on your return.

There is no official discussion of this, but *where* you file your taxes each year may have more of a bearing on whether you are audited than *what* you actually put down on the various lines of your tax return.

For instance, do you live in Los Angeles? If so, it has been demonstrated that you are almost three times more likely to have your tax return audited by the IRS than if you live in Milwaukee or Boston. In fact, the statistics seem to indicate the farther west you live, the better chance you have of being audited. The ten previous steps are designed to minimize your chance of an IRS audit. However, if you are one of the unlucky audit recipients, either by design or luck of the draw, please follow these *ten* commonsense rules during the audit process.

1. Be polite at every step of the process. There will be time to be rude later on if the decision goes against you. However, no matter how mad you become, *never* comment on the auditor's heritage or make threats of any kind; if you do, you *will* be terribly sorry later.

2. Be prepared. Make sure you have all the needed information with you for your appointment the first time. You don't want the IRS to have to schedule a second appointment. It gives them more time to scrutinize your return and ask questions.

3. Make copies of everything—never give them the original to keep.

4. Make all deadlines you are given. If they say they want all data in their office by June 1, they mean June 1, *not* a day later. But nothing says you have to get them in a day earlier either. In fact, some CPAs encourage requesting as many extensions as possible between meetings. The theory: The auditor is under pressure to close your case and open a new one. The more time you take, the more pressure he feels.

5.   Be specific in stating your case. The IRS wants facts, not your opinions. However, I doubt that any living individual really understands the Tax Code. Use this to your advantage.

6.   Get everything in writing! You don't know, over a lengthy process, who you will be talking to next. You may even get a different person every time you talk to them. Build your case with evidence signed by them.

7.   Don't chitchat with the auditor about *anything*—and speak only when spoken to. Nothing good could ever come out of volunteering information to an IRS auditor. In the same spirit, keep all answers short and to the point. Don't ever break the silence with an unnecessary comment. You're likely to say something that can hurt you, such as " I can't wait to get in my new car and make the trip to my condo in Florida for the winter." Not a good idea, especially if you are reporting only $18,000 in last year's income. You will be in for a *long* session.

8.   Never lie during an audit. This could escalate your case to the fraud or criminal division of the IRS. Believe me, this is no place to be. Instead of a penalty that you pull out your checkbook and pay, you could end up in a prison cell for the next few years. Ditto for altering receipts. If you haven't got one, admit that it is lost and move on. And certainly, *never* try to bribe your way out of the situation. This will simply add additional time on to your jail sentence.

9.   Be prepared to pick your battles. If you are assessed with a tax bill that you feel is unfair, or you reach an impasse with your auditor, ask to see his supervisor. At this level, try as hard as you can to work out a compromise with the IRS. Remember, they are there to *close cases;* if you can present a

deal that makes sense, they just may take it. However, if you can't come to terms with the supervisor, think long and hard before you take your next step, which is U.S. Tax Court. The process of developing and presenting a case here is *very* expensive and time consuming; worse, you will rarely win.

10. If an audit seems to be more than you can handle, or you have the funds, consider hiring a CPA (or other qualified individual) to handle the whole audit process. These professionals are very familiar with the audit ordeal; they should know exactly how to best deal with the IRS on most issues. There's another (usually unspoken) advantage to using a representative: If you attend personally, *each time you open your mouth you risk saying something detrimental to your case.* On the other hand, if you are not in attendance, any new questions raised can be answered by your CPA/representative thusly: "I'm not prepared to answer that, as it was not on the original list of questions." Unless it is a major issue, it is likely to be forgotten; again, the auditor is under time restrictions to close your case and move on to the next unfortunate soul.

One final question everybody asks: "How long do I have to keep all this stuff?"

There are two answers to this question: the legal answer and the practical one.

By law, you must keep all personal tax records at least three years from the date you file your tax returns. That is the time frame the IRS has to come knocking on your door looking for more money. However, there are exceptions to the rule. On a return that omitted more than 25 percent of income, the IRS can stretch that time period to six years. If they can prove you filed a false or fraudulent tax return with the intent to cheat them out of their due, there is *no* time limit whatsoever.

The practical response I give my clients is to keep all records for ten years from the date they file the return. (I also warn them not to accidentally throw out records relating to investments or real estate they still may hold even after the ten-year period has expired.) Okay, it's a long time—but how much space can it possibly take up in the attic? Just put the tax return boxes on top of all those old clothes you know you'll never wear again, or the old TV set you never got fixed, or the broken luggage you haven't used in the last twenty years. I think you get the picture.

Good luck—because when it comes to taxes, *everyone* needs it.

Chapter 12

The World of Scams and Con Games:
A Primer for Widows Everywhere

I find it revolting that the very people this book is designed to protect are so often the direct targets of confidence games. Con men everywhere have painted a bull's-eye on the back of every widow, no matter what her wealth or lack thereof. Indeed, it seems the same sad fact is true for *all* honest people, regardless of age, gender, or marital status.

A year or so ago, I hosted a luncheon seminar for all my clients; my guest of honor was the local police chief, who spoke extensively about some of the more prevalent crimes perpetrated on widows and the elderly today. As this book is written, the list keeps expanding. As fast as the police can detect the latest twist, the con man is off and running in a new direction, to a new town, to prey on a new set of victims.

Nobody really knows the total amount of dollars that

are pried from the hands of trusting widows each year. That's because when many widows finally figure out they have been victimized, they are too embarrassed to even report the crime.

Here I detail some of the confidence schemes that law enforcement authorities say are the most common scams being played on the street today.

A note: *Don't think it can't happen to you.*

Intelligent people—of both genders and of all ages— are the prey that these predators target. They're deviously clever, and they use your own honesty and decency against you. If you're not alert to the danger, you very likely will become one of their victims. Your only defense is knowledge. Let's look at some of the ploys they use.

Home Repair Scams

Home repair is the granddaddy of all confidence schemes, especially where widows are involved.

All it takes is a recent copy of the obituaries or a quick trip to your local hall of records to see that your husband is deceased. In a flash, you are fair game. Often, the scam works like this: You are outside one beautiful day, perhaps weeding your garden. Without warning, a man with a huge drum on the back of his truck pulls in your driveway. And an impressive truck it is, too—it's big, with ACME ASPHALT PAVING in large lettering and what looks like a local telephone number prominently displayed below.

Okay, he sure looks awful dirty, but hard work is nothing to be ashamed of, and he certainly sounds polite. He says his howdy and tells you that he just finished up a job two blocks away.

"No offense," he says, and smiles to take the sting from his words. "But I noticed your driveway sure needs some help. It's *way* overdue for seal coating, at the very least."

You nod. "My late husband always took care of that sort of thing."

(Did you hear that? A *cha-CHING!* noise, sort of like a cash register ringing up a big sale? That was the sound of his price for seal coating *doubling.*)

"Well, I'd be glad to handle it for you, ma'am." Then he shakes his head, sadly. "But I'd be less than honest if I didn't tell you the whole story. See all those cracks? And that crumbling spot? Seal coating will only cover them up. A couple of months, the whole thing will probably be rubble."

"Oh, dear. That's terrible."

He nods sympathetically; then maybe he snaps his fingers, as if he had a sudden thought.

"You know, I have just about enough paving material left on my truck to do your driveway. Tell you what: I'll do it—for what the asphalt costs, wholesale—just to keep from having to dump it. I shouldn't, really. But heck, at least this way the company breaks even, and you get your driveway fixed. Is it a deal?"

He quotes $300 for the job, but you negotiate it down to $250. "Okay," he says, "but it has to be in cash." He winks, and by now you may even wink back. After all, you win, he wins; the only loser is the government, which takes too much of your money already.

So you hand over the cash, and from here on the story

changes. Either your industrious friend will be "right back after I grab a little lunch" or he needs to "pick up something I need to finish your job."

Whatever the excuse for leaving, he never returns.

Or even worse, he may *start* the job, tear out a substantial chunk of your driveway, but once you go inside, he is gone. You opted for just the seal coating? You still got no bargain. All he did was apply a thin coat of cheap oil (you don't want to know where he obtained it) that will wash away in the first drizzle.

The story varies, but the outcome is always the same: He gets your money, you get nothing.

Then there are the scams where you actually get work done for you. The problem is, it's work you did not need in the first place. The classic perpetrator (though it is certainly not limited to this trade) is the unscrupulous roofer.

It starts with the first leak, typically on a rainy day. You've cooked your dinner and you're setting a table for one when you notice a wet circle spreading on the ceiling. Fortunately, you kept that flyer you found in the mailbox shortly after your husband died. "Roofing repairs," it says, "reasonable rates, available day or night." Thirty minutes later, he's offering a free estimate and telling you not to worry; it's probably just something both simple and inexpensive to fix. He grabs his ladder and away he goes, to a place you've probably never visited (or wanted to): the roof.

Fifteen minutes later, he's back on the ground with you. "Found the problem over your dining room," he says. "A couple of your roof shingles came loose."

You sigh in relief; it's nothing major, you tell yourself.

And you're right; it is something a good roofer (read: a

competent and honest roofer) could fix in an hour. Total cost to you: no more than, say, $150.

Freeze the videotape here, please.

I repeat: That's the verdict from a *good* roofer—but not this one. While he was doing your "free inspection," he turned your small problem into a big one. As he crossed the roof he simply pulled away other shingles, not only in the trouble spot but strategically, from places where you didn't have problems before. Now you have "a major repair" involving "several other spots" in several other areas.

He can read the expression on your face. Why not? It's the same expression he has seen dozens of times after he has made this same speech. His own expression is thoughtful, and you may think he is calculating repair estimates. Nope; he is *really* calculating just how far he can push the price up before you call another roofer for a competitive bid.

Sadly, I didn't invent this story; I heard it from an intelligent, savvy client who happens to be a widow. In her case, the repair quote came to $1,475. Not a bad profit to fix a $150 problem.

The list is lengthy; if you live long enough, you'll find scam artists in just about every category of home repairman. The TV goes out, there's water in your basement, you look at the peeling paint and think about buying aluminum siding. Or how about window replacement or furnace, air conditioner, washer, or dryer repairs—in all these circumstances, there's no shortage of unscrupulous repair "services."

So how can you tell? And what can you do about it? Here are three points to remember:

1.   Remember: If something seems too good to be true, it probably is. Shop, compare, get competing quotes. Find out what the problem really is and the fair-market cost of fixing it. Never take the first bid; check around before you accept any diagnosis of the problem or agree on a price to fix it.

2.   Start putting together a list of referrals from all your friends of people and companies they have used and with which they are perfectly satisfied. Do this *now,* before you find yourself in need! This way when the occasion arises, you will know who to call—and who to avoid.

3.   Even if you have a good list of reputable repair services, always get three estimates—more, if you have the time. Most often, an honest business will offer you a free estimate on anything that sounds like a major project. Listen; ask questions. If all the bids come out at a similar price, don't always go with the cheapest one. Heed your gut feeling. If a particular repairman or service feels somehow shady to you, go to the next name on your list. But don't count on intuition when someone "feels" like a nice person; at the very least, ask for references—and check them *before* you hire anybody. Also make sure they carry the appropriate liability insurance: Ask to see the details, in writing.

Medical and Health Care Scams

You hear it often from people who want to believe, who are desperate to believe: "There must be a cure somewhere." And sometimes there is; but not always. Each year tens of millions of dollars are wasted on shady medical products and treatments that turn out to be nothing more than updated versions of old Wild West snake oil "cures."

It's tempting to believe that all that ails you—that unsightly, persistent rash, chronic arthritis, the age lines and liver spots—can be cured with a simple and easy-to-use product. To think of all the money you've "wasted" on doctors, hospitals, and their prescription drugs! Because this will cure you, guaranteed—and it costs only $29.95, or $59.95, or some permutation thereof.

Right.

Let's think this through logically. If someone came up with a surefire cure for arthritis, why in the world would they go through the expense and difficulty of marketing, promoting, and manufacturing just to sell it to you for $29.95? Wouldn't every major pharmaceutical company in the world pay big bucks for the secret, if only to keep it from competing with their own "cures"? After they ended up paying me (and my heirs for the next ten generations) enough to live on like kings, would these companies not want to recoup their investment by selling it to you for much more than $29.95?

You bet. And they would—*if it worked*. Is all that logic I mentioned clicking in about now?

Inevitably, a product that sounds too good to be true is precisely that. At best, these scams prove to be nothing more than cheap swindles—harmless, we hope, but not always. The real danger comes in when patients stop taking known, accepted medication and rely on these witches'-brew remedies. Often, this is when the results become more than just a bad joke on gullible people. That's when they can turn deadly.

Financial and Brokerage Scams

It never fails: You just sat down to dinner, and the telephone rings.

You make the mistake of answering it. (Why? Isn't that why they invented caller ID and answering machines?) It's Mr. John Q. Broker of the firm Rip-off Incorporated with the next great investment that is going to make you wealthy beyond your wildest dreams.

It could be a stock, a mutual fund, a real estate deal, or one of a dozen great ideas he has come up with to separate *you* from *your* money. And it works, because most people do indeed answer a ringing phone and are too polite to hang up on even the most persistent salesperson.

Here's what my dear old dad does: turn the tables on them. Ask them, courteously, "Why are you calling me?" Have they called their own mother, father, sister, brother, uncle, or other family member? Insist on an answer here. Did anyone on this list of their own relatives buy it? If so, who? If not, why not? Did any of these people opt to mortgage his or her house to put more in his account? Tell him you really want to see documentation of all these transactions and you might get back to him—but only *after* you receive this information and check out its veracity. To do so, of course, you'll need a list of home phone numbers so you can call and . . .

I hope you are laughing by now, because that's what Dad is always doing when he reaches this point in his story. Usually, the salesman hangs up first; none of them has ever sent Dad the "information" requested. And at least my father has had some fun, even if he ends up reheating dinner.

What usually happens is that Mr. Broker ends up removing Dad's name from his calling list—permanently. And if you're like Dad, this is precisely the result you wanted in the first place.

You may follow my father's example. But even if you don't, *under no circumstances* should you ever, ever send cash, provide credit card numbers, or in any way transfer money to anyone who calls you on the telephone. *Never break this rule!* Again, apply logic: If it is such a great deal, why are they calling *you*? What—did Bill Gates pass on this "sure thing," after telling the phone sales solicitor that he already had enough money?

Logic tells us "probably not."

An interesting variation of this scam comes when a broker buys, say, a list of a thousand names from one of the countless list brokers in this country. The broker will call half the people and tell them XYZ common stock is on the way up; then he'll call the *other* half to warn that the stock is going down. He tells everyone not to do anything—just watch his recommendations to see if he is right is all he asks. He doesn't want you to give him your business now; he wants to earn your business over time.

Naturally, half the recommendations are right and half will be wrong. The half that was right he would call back and repeat the same procedure. The half that was wrong doesn't get called back. This will keep going on several times each time with a new stock until he has maybe fifty people left who have seen nothing but picture-perfect predictions.

By now you have watched countless opportunities slip through your hands. Maybe this guy really does have a crystal ball or has a little Gypsy blood running through his veins. You can't stand it any longer. This guy is a *genius* and you just *have* to jump on the bandwagon . . .

From here one of two things happens, both of them bad. You send him money only to find his recommendations really no better than flipping a coin; he's the kind of broker who makes money by volume trading of other people's money. Or worse, in some cases his brokerage firm doesn't even exist; that check you sent him to improve *your* retirement . . . well, instead you've just added it to *his*.

Bottom line: Don't discuss matters of money over the telephone with anybody you don't know—anytime, anywhere. If one calls and leaves a number, erase it from your answering machine; if you find his business card stuck in your storm door, throw it away immediately.

And while you're at it, throw away all those financial flyers and "sample" investment newsletters you receive in the mail touting documented returns of 200 percent, 300 percent, or 400 percent per year. Think about it for a minute. If someone really knew where a particular stock or the market was going in the future, why would he want to share it with you, at any reasonable price? Wouldn't he make far more money simply by following his own recommendations?

Usually, there is only one person involved who is going to make any money here. Hint: It isn't you.

Check and Checking Account Scams

Checks—if you write them, they will come. The con men, that is.

It is estimated that as a nation we will write somewhere around *65 billion* checks this year. Wherever there is this much of anything going on, someone is certain to learn how to make money from it—and almost always, it will be illegal.

It all starts with the checks we buy. Checks are simple, really: a piece of paper that shows the name of your bank, several typeset lines of required name-and-address information, a few blank spaces, and a long string of cryptic digits along the bottom that repeats most of the above data, though in a numerical manner. You fill in the blanks, sign it, and—presto!—you can use it to transfer money.

In a more innocent age, when you ran out of checks you called the bank and ordered a new supply. But the world has changed. Every Sunday newspaper, some magazines, and all the coupon mailers you receive in the mail have forms for you to fill out and send in to get your refill of checks. And why not? Inevitably, they cost a lot less than what the bank charges.

Ah, but there is a lot of difference between these bargain checks and the more expensive chemical-sensitive checks issued through most banks. With the latter, most attempts to alter them will be readily apparent; it's a problem to chemically erase or otherwise alter them.

But with the cheap ones, any half-smart dishonest person with a minimum of talent can cover the parts of the check he wants to keep (such as your signature) and simply wash the check in an easy-to-obtain chemical called acetone (nail polish remover is over 90 percent acetone). When the laundry is done, all he has to do is fill in the now blank dollar-amount line and payee line with new information—his own name or an alias, for instance, in whatever amount he thinks he can get away with cashing.

Another big mistake involves simple laziness: Many people simply do not fill in the entire name of the payee. Instead, they use an abbreviation. An interesting example occurs each year around April 15, when millions of checks are written to the Internal Revenue Service and dropped in the mail. Try this for fun, but just as an experiment: Write the letters "IRS" on a piece of paper. Now, with just a few strokes of your pen, try to make it say "MRS." As the grand finale, write your own last name after it.

For people who know about the ease with which this can be done, there's a story that may be true or may be one of those urban legends like the alligators that (don't) live in city sewers. It seems that late on the evening of Tax Day, a man in a gray-and-blue uniform shirt stood outside a post office holding a large box and a hand-drawn sign that read PUT TAX FORMS HERE. Car after car driven by last-minute filers would motor right up and do just that.

Have you guessed the end of the story?

Right: The "Postal Service employee" wasn't one; the tax returns (and payment-due checks) he collected were never mailed. Instead, a significant number of procrastinators who looked at their canceled checks a month later were puzzled to find one made out to a "Mrs. Smith."

Oh, yes—in addition to being ripped off for the total

amount of the check, these unfortunates also had the IRS breathing down their backs for their taxes owed *plus* interest and penalties.

So . . .

Some good basic commonsense ideas when dealing with checks are:

1. Always ask for chemical-sensitive, tamper-proof paper when reordering checks.

2. Always fill in the full name of the payee. No abbreviations.

3. Never leave your checks in your mailbox for your mailman to pick up. Always drop them in a secure post office mailbox, give directly to your mailman, or go directly to the post office.

4. Deal only with banking institutions that return your checks to you each month so you can inspect them for signs of foul play.

900-Number Scams

900 Numbers: *There are telephone calls you just shouldn't return, ever.*

You come home from a busy day and check your answering machine. There are the usual messages. The piece of jewelry you dropped off to be fixed is finished; stop by and pick it up anytime. Your son "the big shot" calls; he's running a little short and wonders if you could lend him $200 until payday. The bridge game for Saturday was canceled. Then: "Mrs. Smith, you just won a free trip for two to

Florida for next February! You must call 900-555-1212 by 6:00 P.M. tonight or you will forfeit your prize."

How can this be? Okay, so you don't remember filling out an entry form—but so what? A free trip! Wait until you tell your friends. You pick up the telephone and return the call. The person on the other end is even more excited than you are and seems overjoyed at your good fortune.

"Let me just confirm this," she tells you. "May I put you on hold for a moment?"

You wait for a period that seems to last forever.

You wonder if you've been forgotten, if you should hang up and call again.

And she's back on the line. "Congratulations!" she tells you. "Now, you will receive your official notification in the mail in six to eight weeks, and then you can—"

She goes on for a while longer, chatting about various details. No matter; you just want to hear it again, so you ask one more time: "Are you sure it's me?"

The voice on the phone laughs, delighted. "Oh, yes! You are our winner!"

You're the winner, all right. The winner of a $65 telephone call for the 900 number you just called.

And you're not alone. People like you have been calling in all week from across the country, because they got the same call.

These 900 numbers have been set up so that you are charged for every minute you stay on the line with them, and the fees could be pretty hefty. It's not uncommon for the charges to run $25 for the first minute and $3 a minute for as long as they can keep you on the line.

A few weeks later, you still have not received the mailed details of your "free" vacation. It's not until you receive your telephone bill that a lightbulb goes on above your head. Then you call your telephone company, but it's too late. The line has been disconnected, and your money is gone with it.

Cash Machine Scams

Cash Machines: *Ready cash, 24/7—but for whom?*

By now, most of us understand the appeal of those ubiquitous automated teller machines. There seems to be one on almost every corner these days. Low on cash? Just step up to your friendly cash machine, and the problem is solved. But wherever there is available cash, there will be someone available to take it away from you.

Consider: You use the nearby cash machine; the street is quiet, with no one in sight.

Or so it seemed. You never saw the man in the van sitting across the street with the binoculars reading off your PIN number as you enter it. So you pocket your $50, stopping only to toss your machine-printed receipt in the trash bin near the door. Who needs the extra paper, anyway?

You are around the corner when another person stoops and pulls your crumpled receipt from the trash. He hands the form off to the man in the van, who taps the numbers into a machine the size of a shoebox that is plugged into the car's cigarette lighter outlet. In seconds, he pulls out what looks like a credit card, blank except for the magnetic strip across the back.

Ten minutes later someone else withdraws another $250 from your account using their bogus card and your newfound PIN number.

Unlikely? It happens just this way, every day. Some con men are rumored to place their own garbage can near the cash machine, for your convenience (and theirs). In other real-life cases, the stolen account information and PIN numbers have been used by computer-savvy crooks to electronically transfer money from their victims' accounts into their own, often overseas, banks.

Another common trick is the thief who stuffs a wad of paper or similar material into the machine so that the money you withdraw never makes it down the chute. You curse, perhaps hammer your hand against the metal facing. Then you leave hopping mad, vowing to call the bank the next day to complain about the "broken" machine. As soon as you're out the door, the con man enters, quickly removes his jamming material—and down drops your money—or shall I say *his* money?

But not all crooks want to be creative, or even subtle. These unimaginative types will simply wait until your transaction is completed; if no one else is around, they will proceed with the time-honored tradition of sticking a gun in your face and simply taking your money. There's not much imagination involved here—but as anyone who has looked down the wrong end of a gun barrel will tell you, it can be highly effective.

Banking terminals and cash machines are here to stay. What can *you* do to protect yourself?

I totally avoid using cash stations, and not merely because of the potential for crime. Banks usually don't charge you for an ATM transaction—*if* you use one of their machines. But when do most people usually run out of money? Answer: When they're out of town and away from their own bank and its ATM network. There are high fees associated with using "foreign" ATMs, and I just don't see the benefits.

Not using cash stations isn't always the most convenient choice: I either must make sure I always have enough money on me in the event of an emergency, or I must use a credit card. I advise you to do the same.

But if you must use a cash machine, for whatever purpose, at least find one that is heavily used and located in a high-traffic area. Use your body to conceal the keypad as you enter your PIN. Take all the receipts with you and shred them in a secure location. Before you use the machine, be aware of your surroundings: Is anyone watching you? Is there a telephone at the machine? Does it list a number so that you can notify the relevant authority if the machine malfunctions?

Tenants and House Partner Scams

"But I thought she was my friend!"

Many times after the loss of a spouse, the topic may turn to whether or not you should open the doors of your home to a tenant or house partner. Sometimes it is out of loneliness and other times it is out of financial necessity. It could be a great decision or your worst nightmare—and I don't mean because of incompatibility.

There are people out there that make a living being a

professional tenant. Take this example. You're finishing your shopping at the local supermarket and before you leave the store, you read the local bulletin board as you sometimes do. Let's see, there are ads for dogs for sale, baby-sitter services, rent-a-husband odd-job repairs, cars for sale—all the same ones from last week.

Wait! There *is* a new one: "Widow, 55, new to the area. Seeks same to share house/apartment for companionship, dinners out, and mutual financial savings."

Taking a tenant is not a new thought for you. It has been rather lonely around the house since John died; you do have three extra bedrooms; and sharing expenses wouldn't hurt either.

So you call the hotel where she is staying. She sounds reasonable, and you make arrangements for her to visit your house to determine how well the two of you might get along. You're naturally skeptical but after about an hour together, you would swear she and you were good friends. How could this be? Something in the cosmos must have aligned just right.

She lost her husband about two years ago, the same as you. She likes to stay up and watch old movies; so do you. Her favorite food is Mexican; so is yours. You enjoy jack-lighting muskie on cold winter nights on Lake Superior; eerily, so does she. *This is just too good to be true,* you tell yourself.

In every way, she sounds great; you decide to take the plunge. The extra money will be a godsend, it'll be nice to have someone around to talk to, and you see this as the beginning of a lifelong friendship.

Sadly, the friendship has a *very* short life. Six months

later, you come home from a weekend of visiting the kids to find your furniture, jewelry, TV, and just about everything else of value is gone. Not surprisingly, so is your caring house partner.

It happens more often than you think.

For that reason, if you are going to invite someone to share your house, do an extensive background check, including a copy of her credit report (you'll need her signed permission to do this). If the person is legitimate, she should have no problem giving you all the information you need. If she objects, pass.

What should you look for in this background check? Obviously, a criminal record is a deal breaker; in most cases, so is a history of credit or financial problems. Personal references are an absolute *must;* get them, call them, check them. Does your prospective tenant have children, or any family of her own nearby? If so, try to meet them. Unless there are family disputes involved, you're likely to deal with them on occasion, at least as visitors to your house. Are they compatible with you?

Even if your tenant doesn't turn out to be a kleptomaniac or Charlie Manson's daughter, you need to take one more precaution to protect yourself: Get everything in writing, preferably in the form of a "lease document."

A lease will detail up-front such points as the amount of monthly rent, when rent is due, how utilities and other shared expenses are to be paid, limitations on behavior (i.e., no pit bulls or sex-crazed visitors allowed, at least not after 9:00 P.M.), the term of the lease (six months, a year, etc.), any late fees or penalties that may be incurred and—*most important!*—under what terms you can throw her out legally if she doesn't conform to the rules you have set.

Always ask for a security deposit of two months' rent, paid in advance upon the lease signing. Two months' worth protects you (tenants often love to stick landlords for the last month's rent, commonly by saying "Use the deposit for the last month's rent." Uh-huh—until you find that she tore out the wall between her two rooms "for easier access."

And always inform your insurance agent—in advance—that you're taking in a tenant. Your homeowner's policy may not cover rentals, or it may limit coverage in the event of accidents in your home by a tenant. Inform your tenant that she will need her own renter's insurance to protect her personal property; ask to see the policy and get a copy for your records.

Finally, if you live in a condominium, town house, or a residence with a strict homeowners' association, check with them in advance to make sure there are no provisions or ordinances restricting you from taking in a tenant.

Bank Scams

Bank Scams: *"I only wanted to help . . ."*

This scam is as old as the hills. But because it keeps working, con men keep running it—and making money from it. It begins as a normal day for some unsuspecting soul—a soul, in fact, much like yours. You start the day off running your daily errands—grocery store, dry cleaner's, and so on—but this is also your banking day. You need to make a deposit and get some cash. Despite the personal loss, life has been relatively benign for you since your husband died. The house is paid off; you were able to afford that new car; and you finally feel that your life is returning to normal.

But today, as you park your new car outside the bank, you didn't notice the two men sitting in the car next to you. You conduct your business and head straight home to put your groceries away. But the car with the two men from the bank follows you home.

An hour later, the doorbell rings; you find two very official-looking men standing in your doorway. One even has a badge, while the other shows you a business card that identifies him as a senior vice president of your bank. They introduce themselves and state they need your help.

"We think one of our people at the bank is embezzling money," the VP tells you. He nods at the policeman. "The authorities are investigating, of course—but they can't prove it, and we need your help."

How exciting! As one of their best customers, they ask you to withdraw $9,500, come outside, and give them the money.

"We'll mark the bills," the policeman said. "Then one of our people will return and deposit the money. When our thief takes the bait, we'll have him red-handed."

You feel heroic and flattered. You may even get on TV when this is over.

So you do exactly as they say. And then you go home to wait; the nice man from the bank promised to call you with all the details of the arrest. And you never see your money again.

There are all kinds of names for these kinds of confidence scams. Many of them are predicated on the desire of civic-minded people to do good; others count on the need for adventure that so many of us share.

It's sad, but the lesson here is not to trust anyone—*anyone!*—when it comes to your money. Catching crooks is not an endeavor that either a bank or a police department would entrust to an untrained civilian. Even more telling, no bank would risk the potential liability involved in asking a depositor to risk her own funds in such a manner. (Think logically: Doesn't the bank have enough of its own money to use?) Had she not been carried forward by her own desire to assist (and for her own instinct for adventure), our widow would have realized that the proposition made to her simply made no sense—at least, not in the real world.

She would have done what anyone should do if approached with an unusual or illogical request from the "authorities." Call the police immediately; call the bank, and ask for the head of security. Know that the real police department and your local bank would never put you through such an ordeal.

Credit Card Scams

"I don't have that kind of money."
It started out as such a beautiful Monday morning—if there *is* such a thing as a beautiful *Monday* morning. You stroll to the mailbox to pick up your mail, not a care in the world. Nothing unusual here: a couple of magazines, advertisements.

Oh, yes—and your monthly Visa bill has arrived.

Not too many years before, the arrival of the Visa bill was enough to send your heartbeat into hyperdrive, largely because you could never remember what you spent or where you spent it over the last month. But no more; ever since you started saving all those credit-card receipts and putting money away to pay the bill, Visa holds no terrors for you.

Or so you thought.

This time, you notice the envelope feels thicker and heavier than usual. You rip open the envelope, thinking, *They must have enclosed a lot of those little sales pages in this month trying to get me to buy—*

A-H-H-H-H-H-H-H-H!!!

The monthly total of your charges comes to $6,851.28!?!

Someone, somehow, somewhere obtained the information on your card. Maybe he used it himself; more likely, he sold the information to someone else who used it to charge purchases to *your* card. Either way, to all appearances, someone had a helluva shopping spree, on *your* account.

How they got the information is an ever-changing game of electronic cops-and-robbers. It could have been the most recent purchase you made on the Internet. The World Wide Web is the modern-day version of No Man's Land. Despite security technology, crooks regularly pluck credit card numbers from cyberspace. Or it might have been when you made a purchase from the late-night infomercial on TV. Or from one of the restaurants you visited, or the airplane ticket you bought, or the car you rented, or . . .

Recently, I went to a clinic I had not visited before, for a routine blood screening—just to make certain all the numbers were in the proper ranges. I arrived five minutes after the office opened, and the waiting room was already crowded. One by one, each person in line ahead of me was called to the reception window and asked—loudly and clearly—for his or her Social Security number, date and place of birth, home address, phone number, and so on. If anybody with crime on his mind had been taking notes, life could have become very complicated for all the patients there that day.

Today the bad guys have the technology, the access, the opportunity; all they need is your card number and expiration date to start the cards a-charging.

Luckily for you and your fellow credit card holders, most of what these thieves steal won't come from your personal pocket. Believe me, your credit card company will investigate before it lets you off the hook. But even in a worst-case scenerio, federal law limits your own liability to a maximum of $100 (or even zero dollars, if you've signed up for one of the fraud-protection plans that card companies offer for a fee). Sometimes, and particularly if you have been a good customer, the credit card issuer may even waive any charge.

So who does pay? The simple answer: The issuer of the card is responsible for the loss. But as with most things of this nature, indirectly we all pay. We pay through higher prices, the margin that merchants build in to buffer any losses from fraud; we pay through the higher rates and fees the credit card company builds in for the same reason.

The different ways and means of credit card fraud could fill a book in itself. Suffice it to say, watch your credit cards like a mother hen watches her chicks.

Two more essential tips:

1.   If your card has expired, use a scissors to cut the old one up in *several* pieces—the more, the better. When I destroy mine, the first cut is through the line that has my account number; I go straight down the center of the numbers. After that, I become creative: a diagonal cut here, a curving cut there. It's time for slice-and-dice. If someone is going to go through your garbage to steal your old credit card information (don't laugh; it happens), make them work for it.

2.   Always rip, shred, and ruthlessly mutilate all those applications you receive in the mail inviting you to apply for new cards that you probably don't want anyway. It is child's play for a thief to fill out a discarded form; all he needs to do is report that "you" have moved and have the new card sent to a different address: his.

Identity Scams

Identity theft—*pray it never happens to you.* This one is so scary there have actually been movies based on this theme. It's the dark gift that keeps on giving, if your idea of a Christmas present is a box of anthrax.

This is not a onetime thing that you can shrug off, where you can say that you learned a valuable lesson, laugh about being so naïve, and get on with your life. This is the crime that will *rock* your universe, right down to the depths of your soul.

In essence, what happens with identity theft is someone actually *becomes* you; whatever they do for their own financial gain becomes part of what your teachers once called your permanent record. They take out a loan? It's in *your* name. They decide to apply for a passport? Rob a bank? Get married to one—or more—gullible partners? Every computer file that bears your name will swear to the bottom of its electronic heart that *you* are the evildoer.

The true culprit may not know you from Adam. All he is looking for is a free ride on the coattails of an innocent who is approximately his own age and gender.

How does it start? Have you ever filled out a credit application for a new department store credit card, new car loan, or other loan application? Social Security number, date and place of birth, home address, employment information—perhaps even your mother's maiden name: right there, on a piece of paper that could end up anywhere, is everything a person needs to become *you*.

Here's an even scarier thought: An enterprising crook could likely find the same information by rummaging through your garbage, or by Dumpster diving for discarded employee files at your place of employment. It's improbable you would even know your ID has been stolen.

Armed with this information, the initial step is for the criminal to get a copy of your birth certificate. In most states, this is ridiculously easy. He simply pays a few dollars for a certified copy, and the birth certificate is sent to him, with no questions asked.

From there they are off to the races. They can now get

legitimate credentials on their own—a driver's license, credit cards, passport—anything they need to literally become you. They keep ringing up the bills in your name, and you are left holding the bag.

Will they get caught? Maybe yes—but probably no. Much depends on how competent they are and how long they prey on *your* name before moving on to their next victim.

When credit theft occurs, there is no simple recourse. This is a problem that could take years (and thousands of dollars) with still no guarantee you will be able to clear your own name. Computers are without souls and bereft of mercy; once something gets into the official record, it may never come out. Meanwhile, your credit rating is devastated, no one short of a Mafia loan shark will consider you for a loan of any size, and your world is turned inside out.

The best defense is prevention: Guard your personal financial information closely, shred or tear up old information you plan on throwing away. And, most important, check your credit history—*often*. God forbid, if some low-life steals your identity, it may be the only chance you have to nip the nightmare in the bud.

Identity Theft: It *Can* Happen to You

Attorney General John Ashcroft calls identity theft "one of the fastest growing crimes in the United States." The Privacy Rights Clearinghouse, an independent agency that tracks ID theft as well as other privacy-related issues, estimates that 500,000 to 700,000 cases are reported annually.

And the ingenuity of identity thieves is boundless. For instance, in 2002 indictments were returned on three Detroit men who assumed the identities of elderly homeowners and convinced banks and mortgage companies to issue them loans against the properties they "owned." When the trio defaulted on the loans, the mortgage holders foreclosed—on homes in which, in most instances, the actual owner was still residing, unaware of the fraud.

Here are a few other recent examples of the vulnerability we all now share:

- Three Detroit men were charged with using stolen identity information and an official form to execute $1.7 million in stock options owned by a retired K mart executive.
- A health insurance plan's former employee stole personal information on fifteen people insured by his employer and offered it for sale at $1,000 per person.
- A ring of at least fifteen people ran up $1.5 million in charges on other people's credit cards over five years, buying designer clothes and fancy purses. Fourteen have pleaded guilty.
- A former manager of a car rental company traded information customers had provided when renting to the manager of a Troy escort service, in exchange for time with the women who worked there. The escort manager ran up $260,000 in credit card charges before he was caught.

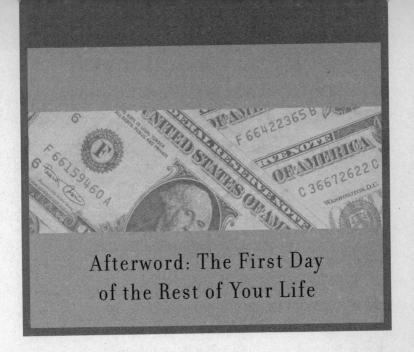

Afterword: The First Day of the Rest of Your Life

I drove to my office this morning; it was a beautiful early-summer day. The sun was shining, warm and bright and high in a robin's-egg sky. The faintest hint of a breeze riffled through the boughs of the trees, not unlike a mother's hand caressing the hair of her child.

At such moments, it is easy to imagine that God's in His heaven and all is well in the world.

For some—the fortunate among us—that is, in fact, an undeniable truth. These lucky souls are our fellow travelers who have avoided the tragedies, both large and small, that darken the lives of so many others. These fortunate few have discovered secret ways to look past the difficult or the mundane, and to focus on those endeavors which bring them joy and pleasure.

But for many people—probably, for most of you who

are reading this book—the sun is not always shining, nor are the winds of fate always fair.

You have learned much. Through a profound loss, you have discovered that the ability to endure each day can itself be what passes for a small victory of life.

But in the course of reading *Financial Strategies for Today's Widow,* I hope you have learned something else, too: that you are neither alone nor without the promise of a better future. Nothing can minimize the loss you have endured, but a remarkable feature of the human creature is that she can *heal.* And does, as I also hope you've seen from the stories I've brought you in this book.

Regardless of their ages, backgrounds, or the particular circumstances in which they found themselves widows, the women in this book share a characteristic common to their gender: They are possessed of hidden reserves of strength and personal resolve into which they tap at times of crisis—often, without previously knowing that these wellsprings even existed inside themselves.

The women of this book came to me for help—but not because they needed a protector, or desired to in some way subjugate their lives to the dictates of another. Indeed, the majority of them came to me because, in the dawning awareness of their own changed circumstances, they saw both the need *and* the opportunity to learn how to take control of their own destinies.

Much of what I have written deals with the financial decisions they, and you, must now make. But I hope you have also discerned that taking charge of their finances was only part of what the widows of this book accomplished.

In each case, they redefined themselves in far more profound ways.

As I write this, there are slightly more than 12 million widows aged eighteen or older living in the United States; that is almost 11 percent of the country's adult population. And while all of them are linked by the definition of their widowhood, each of them—each of *you*—is far more than a mere demographic category could describe.

Recently I read about Beatrice Muller, who, in January 2000 at age eighty-two and after the death of her husband the previous year, moved into cabin 4068 on deck 4 of the *Queen Elizabeth II*. It was, she decided, a better value than living in a retirement home. She did the math: For what she wanted, each would cost around $5,000 a month. On the luxury liner, meals are inclusive.

But do any of us really believe that she made her decision solely on a dollars-and-cents basis? Since moving aboard, Beatrice has cruised the world; by August 2001, she had chalked up her thirtieth crossing of the Atlantic Ocean. As she told reporters at that time, the life she found on the *QEII* is "enough for me. I have everything I need here." And while she admitted to the occasional loneliness, she added: "If I had been home, I probably wouldn't have been alive."

Clearly, not all of us would make the same choice she did; not all of us could, for a variety of personal and financial reasons.

But perhaps the most important message from Beatrice's story—and from the stories of the widows you've met in this book—is that each of you has the ability to take charge. You can reshape your life, both personal and financial, into a form that fits your desires as well as your needs.

All you need is two things: first, the *will* to do it; second, the *tools* to help you in your quest.

My wholehearted wish is that this book provides you with the latter.

My sincere belief is that, because it was your decision to read this book, you already had all you need of the first.

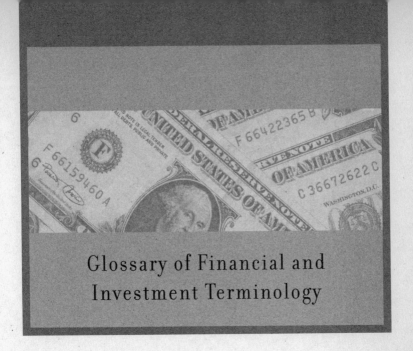

Glossary of Financial and Investment Terminology

Throughout this book, I've tried to keep the language as straightforward as possible. Still, much of it is about finance, investments, and other complex topics. I've tried to explain terms as I write, but in the interest of making sure you can follow some of the more arcane terminology, the glossary below may be of assistance.

Account (in general): contractual relationship between a buyer and seller under which payment is made at a later time. The term *open account* or *charge account* is used, depending on whether the relationship is commercial or personal.

Account Executive: brokerage firm employee who advises and handles orders for clients and has the legal powers of an *agent*. Every account executive must pass certain tests and be registered with the National Association of Securities Dealers (NASD) before soliciting orders from customers; also called *registered representative*.

Accumulated Dividend: dividend due, usually to holders of cumulative preferred stock, but not paid. It is carried on the books as a liability until paid.

Actuary: mathematician employed by an insurance company to calculate premiums, reserves, dividends, and insurance, pension, and annuity rates, using risk factors obtained from experience tables. These tables are based on both the company's history of insurance claims and other industry and general statistical data.

Administrator: court-appointed individual or bank charged with carrying out the court's decisions with respect to a decedent's estate until it is fully distributed to all claimants. Administrators are appointed when a person dies without having made a will or without having named an executor, or when the named executor cannot or will not serve. The term *administratrix* is sometimes used if the individual appointed is a woman. In a general sense, an administrator is a person who carries out an organization's policies.

Amendment: addition to, or change in, a legal document. When properly signed, it has the full legal effect of the original document.

Amortization: accounting procedure that gradually reduces the cost value of a limited-life or intangible asset through periodic charges to income. For fixed assets the term used is *depreciation*, and for wasting assets (natural resources) it is depletion. Both terms mean essentially the same thing as *amortization*.

Analyst: person in a brokerage house, bank trust department, or mutual-fund group who studies a number of companies and makes buy or sell recommendations on the securities of particular companies and industry groups. Most analysts specialize in a particular industry, but some investigate any company that interests them, regardless of its business. Some analysts have considerable influence and can therefore affect the price of a company's stock when they issue a buy or sell recommendation.

Annual Meeting: once-a-year meeting when the managers of a company report to stockholders on the year's results and the board of directors stands for election for the next year. The chief executive officer usually comments on the outlook for the coming year and, with other senior officers, answers questions from shareholders. Stockholders can also request that resolutions on corporate policy be voted on by all those owning stock in the company. Stockholders unable to attend the annual meeting may vote for directors and pass on resolutions through the use of proxy material, which must legally be mailed to all shareholders of record.

Annual Report: yearly record of a corporation's financial condition that must be distributed to shareholders under Securities and Exchange Commission regulations. Included in the report is a description of the company's operations as well as its balance sheet and income statement.

Annuity: form of contract sold by life insurance companies that guarantees a fixed or variable payment to the annuitant at some future time, usually retirement. In a *fixed annuity,* the amount will ultimately be paid out in regular installments varying only with the payout method elected. In a *variable annuity,* the payout is based on a guaranteed number of units; unit values and payments depend on the value of the underlying investments. All capital in the annuity grows tax-deferred. Key considerations when buying an annuity are the financial soundness of the insurance company, the returns it has paid in the past, and the level of fees and commissions paid to salesmen.

Appreciation: increase in the value of an asset such as a stock, bond, commodity, or real estate.

Asset: anything having commercial or exchange value that is owned by a business, institution, or individual.

Asset Allocation: apportioning of investment funds among categories of assets, such as cash equivalents, stock, fixed-income investments, and such tangible assets as real estate, precious metals, and collectibles. Also applies to subcategories such as government, municipal, and corporate bonds, and industry groupings of common stocks. Asset allocation affects both risk and return. It is a central concept in personal financial planning and investment management.

Asset-backed Securities: bonds or notes backed by loan paper or accounts receivable originated by banks, credit card companies, or other providers of credit and often "enhanced" by a bank letter of credit or by insurance coverage provided by an institution other than the issuer. Typically, the originator of the loan or accounts receivable paper sells it to a specially created trust, which repackages it as securities with a minimum denomination of $1,000 and a term of five years or less. The securities are then underwritten by brokerage firms, which reoffer them to the public.

At Risk: exposed to the danger of loss. Investors in a limited partnership can claim tax deductions only if they can prove that there's a chance of never realizing any profit and of losing their investment as well. Deductions will be disallowed if the limited partners are not exposed to economic risk—if, for example, the general partner guarantees to return all capital to limited partners even if the business venture should lose money.

At the Close: order to buy or sell a security within the final thirty seconds of trading. Brokers never guarantee that such orders will be executed.

At the Money: at the current price, as an option with an exercise price equal to or near the current price of the stock or underlying futures contract.

At the Opening: customer's order to a broker to buy or sell a security at the price that applies when an exchange opens. If the order is not executed at that time, it is automatically canceled.

Audit: professional examination and verification of a company's accounting documents and supporting data for the purpose of rendering an opinion as to their fairness, consistency, and conformity with generally accepted accounting principles.

Back-end Load: redemption charge an investor pays when withdrawing money from an investment. Most common in mutual funds and annuities, the back-end load is designed to discourage withdrawals. Also called *deferred sales charge, exit fee, redemption charge*.

Balanced Mutual Fund: fund that buys common stock, preferred stock, and bonds in an effort to obtain the highest return consistent with a low-risk strategy. A balanced fund typically offers a higher yield than a pure stock fund and performs better than such a fund when stocks are falling. In a rising market, however, a balanced mutual fund usually will not keep pace with all-equity funds.

Bankruptcy: state of insolvency of an individual or an organization; an inability to pay debts. There are two kinds of legal bankruptcy under U.S. law: *involuntary,* when one or more creditors petition to have a debtor judged insolvent by a court; and *voluntary,* when the debtor brings the petition. In both cases, the objective is an orderly and equitable settlement of obligations.

Bank Trust Department: part of a bank engaged in settling estates, administering trusts and guardianships, and performing agency services. As part of its personal trust and estate planning services, it manages investments for large accounts—typically those with at least $50,000 in assets. People who cannot or do not want to make investment decisions are commonly bank trust department clients.

Bear Market: prolonged period of falling prices. A bear market in stocks is usually brought on by the anticipation of declining economic activity, and a bear market in bonds is caused by rising interest rates.

Beneficiary: there are five types of beneficiaries:

    1.   person to whom an inheritance passes as the result of being named in a will;

    2.   recipient of the proceeds of a life insurance policy;

    3.   party in whose favor a letter of credit is issued;

    4.   party to whom the amount of an annuity is payable;

    5.   party for whose benefit a trust exists.

Best's Rating: rating of financial soundness given to insurance companies by Best's Rating Service. The top rating is A++. A. M. Best's rating is important to buyers of insurance or annuities because it informs them whether a company is financially sound. Best's Ratings are also important to investors in insurance stocks.

Bid and Asked: *bid* is the highest price a prospective buyer is prepared to pay at a particular time for a trading unit of a given security; *asked* is the lowest price acceptable to a prospective seller of the same security.

U.S. Treasury Bill: commonly called *bill* or *T-bill* by money market people, a Treasury bill is a short-term (maturities up to a year), discounted government security sold through competitive bidding at weekly and monthly auctions in denomination from $10,000 to $1 million.

Black Friday: day on which a historically significant sharp drop in a financial market occurred. The original Black Friday was September 24, 1869, when a group of financiers tried to corner the gold market and precipitated a business panic followed by a depression. The panic of 1873 also began on Friday, and Black Friday has come to apply to any debacle affecting the financial markets.

Black Monday: October 19, 1987, when the Dow Jones Industrial Average plunged a record 508 points following sharp drops the previous week, which reflected investor anxiety about inflated stock price levels, federal budget and trade deficits, and foreign market activity. Many blamed computerized, automated program trading for the extreme volatility.

Blue Chip: common stock of a nationally known company that has a long record of profit growth and dividend payment and a reputation for quality management, products, and services. These stocks are typically high priced and low yielding.

Boiler Room: place where high-pressure salespeople use banks of telephones to call lists of potential investors (known in the trade as *sucker lists*) in order to peddle speculative, even fraudulent, securities.

Bond: any interest-bearing or discounted government or corporate security that obligates the issuer to pay the bondholder a specified sum of money, usually at specific intervals, and to repay the principal amount of the loan at maturity. Bondholders have an IOU from the issuer, but no corporate ownership privileges, as stockholders do.

Bond Rating: method of evaluating the possibility of default by a bond issuer. Standard & Poor's, Moody's Investors Service, and Fitch Investors Service analyze the financial strength of each bond's issuer, whether a corporation or a government body. Their ratings range from AAA (highly unlikely to default) to D (in default). Bonds rated BB or below are not investment grade; in other words, under most state laws, institutions that invest other people's money may not buy them.

Broker:

Insurance: person who finds the best insurance deal for a client and then sells the policy to the client.

Real Estate: person who represents the seller and gets a commission when the property is sold.

Securities: person who acts as an intermediary between a buyer and seller, usually charging a commission. A broker who specializes in stocks, bonds, commodities, or options acts as an agent and must be registered with the exchange on which the securities are traded. Hence the term *registered representative*.

Bull: person who thinks prices will rise. One can be bullish on the prospects for an individual stock, bond, or commodity; an industry segment; or the market as a whole. In a more general sense, *bullish* means optimistic, so a person can be bullish on the economy as a whole.

Bull Market: prolonged rise in the prices of stocks, bonds, or commodities. Bull markets usually last at least a few months and are characterized by high trading volume.

Buy: acquire property in return for money. *Buy* can be used as a synonym for *bargain*.

Capital Gain: difference between an asset's purchase price and selling price when the difference is positive.

Capital Loss: amount by which the proceeds from the sale of a capital asset are less than the cost of acquiring it.

Cash: asset account on a balance sheet representing paper currency and coins, negotiable money orders and checks, and bank balances.

Certificate of Deposit (CD): debt instrument issued by a bank that usually pays interest. Institutional CDs are issued in denominations of $100,000 or more; individual CDs start as low as $100. Maturities range from a few weeks to several years. Interest rates are set by competitive forces in the marketplace.

Certified Public Accountant (CPA): accountant who has passed certain exams, achieved a certain amount of experience, reached a certain age, and met all other statutory and licensing requirements of the state in which he or she works. In addition to accounting and auditing, CPAs prepare tax returns for corporations and individuals.

Commission:

 Real Estate: percentage of the selling price of the property, paid by the seller.

 Securities: fee paid to a broker for executing a trade based on the number of shares traded or the dollar amount of the trade. Since 1975, when regulation ended, brokers have been free to charge whatever they like.

Common Stock: units of ownership of a public corporation. Owners typically are entitled to vote on the selection of directors and other important matters as well as to receive dividends on their holdings.

Condominium: form of real estate ownership in which individual residents hold a deed and title to their houses or apartments and pay a maintenance fee to a management company for the upkeep of common property such as grounds, lobbies, and elevators as well as other amenities.

Corporate Bond: debt instrument issued by a private corporation, as distinct from one issued by a government agency or a municipality. Corporate bonds typically have four distinguishing features:

1. They are taxable;
2. They have a par value of $1,000;
3. They have a term maturity—which means they come due all at once—and are paid for out of a sinking fund accumulated for that purpose;
4. They are traded on major exchanges, with prices published in newspapers.

Credit Rating: formal evaluation of an individual's or company's credit history and capability of repaying obligations.

Day Trade: purchase and sale of a position during the same day.

Diversification: spreading risk by putting assets in several categories of investments—stocks, bonds, money market instruments, and precious metals, for instance—or several industries; or a mutual fund, with its broad range of stocks in one portfolio.

Dividend: distribution of earnings to shareholders, prorated by class of security and paid in the form of money, stock, scrip, or, rarely, company products or property.

Estate: all the assets a person possesses at the time of death, such as securities, real estate, interests in business, physical possessions, and cash. The estate is distributed to heirs according to the dictates of the person's will or, if there is no will, a court ruling.

Estate Planning: planning for the orderly handling, disposition, and administration of an estate when the owner dies. Estate planning includes drawing up a will, setting up trusts, and minimizing estate taxes, perhaps by passing property to heirs before death.

Estate Tax: tax imposed by a state or the federal government on assets left to heirs in a will.

Family of Funds: group of mutual funds managed by the same investment management company.

Financial Planner: professional who analyzes personal financial circumstances and prepares a program to meet financial needs and objectives.

Foreclosure: process by which a homeowner who has not made timely payments of principal and interest on a mortgage loses title to the home.

Gift Tax: graduated tax levied on the donor of a gift by the federal government and most state governments when assets are passed from one person to another.

Index Fund: mutual fund whose portfolio matches that of a broad-based index such as Standard & Poor's Index and whose performance theoretically mirrors the market as a whole.

Inflation: rise in the prices of goods and services, as happens when spending increases relative to the supply of goods on the market.

Interest:
    1.   Cost of using money, expressed as a rate per period of time, usually one year, in which case it is called an *annual rate of interest;*
    2.   Share, right, or title in property.

Jumbo Certificate of Deposit: certificate with a minimum denomination of $100,000. Jumbo CDs are usually bought and sold by large institutions such as banks, pension funds, money market funds, and insurance companies.

Junk Bond: bond with a credit rating of BB or lower by rating agencies.

Load: sales charge paid by an investor who buys shares in a load mutual fund or annuity.

Load Fund: mutual fund that is sold for a sales charge by a brokerage firm or other sales representative.

Margin Call: demand that a customer deposit enough money or securities to bring a margin account up to the initial margin or minimum maintenance requirements.

Money Market Fund: open-ended mutual fund that invests in commercial paper, banker's acceptances, repurchase agreements, government securities, certificates of deposit, and other highly liquid and safe securities, and pays money market rates of interest.

Municipal Bond: debt obligation of a state or local government entity.

Mutual Fund: Fund operated by an investment company that raises money from shareholders and invests it in stocks, bonds, options, commodities, or money market securities. These funds offer investors the advantages of diversification and professional management.

NASDAQ: the NASDAQ Composite Index is a broad-based capitalization-weighted index of all NASDAQ National Market and Small Cap stocks. The index was developed with a base level of 100 as of February 5, 1971.

New York Stock Exchange (NYSE): oldest (1792) and largest stock exchange in the United States, located at 11 Wall Street in New York City; also known as the Big Board and the Exchange.

No-load Fund: mutual fund offered by an open-end investment company that imposes no sales charge (*load*) on its shareholders.

Over the Counter (OTC): security that is not listed and traded on an organized exchange.

Prospectus: formal written offer to sell securities that sets forth the plan for a proposed business enterprise or the facts concerning an existing one that an investor needs to make an informed decision.

Real Estate Investment Trust (REIT): company, usually traded publicly, that manages a portfolio of real estate to earn profits for shareholders.

Rollover: movement of funds from one investment to another. For instance, an individual retirement account may be rolled over when a person retires into an annuity or other form of pension plan payout system. When a bond or certificate of deposit matures, the funds may be rolled over into another bond or certificate of deposit.

Sales Charge: fee paid to a brokerage house by a buyer of shares in a load mutual fund or a limited partnership.

Savings Bond: U.S. Government bond issued in face value denominations ranging from $50 to $10,000.

Securities: relationship between a broker-dealer firm and its client wherein the firm, through its registered representatives, acts as agent in buying and selling securities and sees to related administrative matters.

Short-term Gain or Loss: for tax purposes, the profit or loss realized from the sale of securities or other capital assets held six months or less.

Single-premium Deferred Annuity (SPDA): tax-deferred investment similar to an individual retirement account, without many of the IRA restrictions. An investor makes a lump-sum payment to an insurance company or mutual fund selling the annuity. That lump sum can be invested in either a *fixed-return* instrument like a CD or a *variable-return* portfolio that can be switched among stocks, bonds, and money market accounts. Proceeds are taxed only when distributions are taken. In contrast to an IRA, there is no limit to the amount that may be invested in an SPDA. Like the IRA, the tax penalty for withdrawals before age 59½ is 10 percent.

Split: increase in a corporation's number of outstanding shares of stock without any change in the shareholder's equity or aggregate market value at the time of the split.

Standard & Poor's Index: broad-based measurement of changes in stock-market conditions based on the average performance of 500 widely held common stocks; commonly known as the Standard & Poor's 500 (or S&P 500).

Stock Certificate: documentation of a shareholder's ownership in a corporation. Stock certificates are engraved intricately on heavy paper to deter forgery. They indicate the number of shares owned by an individual, their par value (if any), the class of stock (for example, common or preferred), and attendant voting rights.

Stock Dividend: payment of a corporate dividend in the form of stock rather than cash. The stock dividend may be additional shares in the company, or it may be shares in a subsidiary being spun off to shareholders.

Stock Exchange: organized marketplace in which stocks, common stock equivalents, and bonds are traded by members of the exchange, acting both as agents (brokers) and as principals (dealers and traders).

Tax Bracket: point on the income-tax rate schedules where taxable income falls; also called marginal tax bracket. It is expressed as a percentage to be applied to each additional dollar earned over the base amount for that bracket. Under a progressive tax system, increases in taxable income lead to higher marginal rates in the form of higher brackets.

Tax Deferred: term describing an investment whose accumulated earnings are free from taxation until the investor takes possession of them.

Tax Shelter: method used by investors to legally avoid or reduce tax liabilities.

Testamentary Trust: trust created by a will, as distinguished from an *inter vivos trust,* which is created during the lifetime of the grantor.

Total Return: annual return on an investment including appreciation and dividends or interest.

Treasuries: negotiable debt obligations of the U.S. government, secured by its full faith and credit and issued at various schedules and maturities.

Trust: fiduciary relationship in which a person, called a *trustee,* holds title to property for the benefit of another person, called a *beneficiary.*

Unit Investment Trust: investment vehicle, registered with the SEC under the Investment Company Act of 1940, that purchases a fixed portfolio of income-producing securities, such as corporate, municipal, or government bonds, mortgage-backed securities, or preferred stock.

Variable Annuity: life insurance annuity contract whose value fluctuates with that of an underlying securities portfolio or other index of performance. The variable annuity contrasts with a *conventional* or *fixed* annuity, whose rate of return is constant and therefore vulnerable to the effects of inflation. Income on a variable annuity may be taken periodically, beginning immediately or at any future time. The annuity may be a single-premium or multiple-premium contract.

Wall Street: common name for the financial district at the lower end of Manhattan in New York City, where the New York and American Stock Exchanges and numerous brokerage firms are headquartered. The New York Stock Exchange is actually located at the corner of Wall and Broad streets.

Wire House: national or international brokerage firm whose branch offices are linked by a communications system that permits the rapid dissemination of prices, information, and research relating to financial markets and individual securities.

Write-off: charging an asset amount to expense or loss. The effect of a write-off is to reduce or eliminate the value of the asset and reduce profits.

Zero-coupon Security: security that makes no periodic interest payments but instead is sold at a deep discount from its face value. The buyer of such a bond receives the rate of return by the gradual appreciation of the security, which is redeemed at face value on a specified maturity date.

Index

Accountants, 50, 82–83
Account-churning, 67, 76, 84
Actuarial table, 143
Annual income, in budget, 106
Annual percentage fees, 75, 76
Annuities, 34–36
ATM transactions, 254–56
Audits, tax, 234–38
Automobiles, 191–213
  financing, 207–10
  insurance, 139, 161
  leasing, 196–202
  on-line buying, 208
  options, 202–3
  prices, 203–5
  three rules of car buying, 211–13
  trade-ins, 206–7

Bank accounts, 49, 51
Bank scams, 259–61
Beneficiary, 44, 181
Bequests, 157–58, 183, 185
Brokerage houses, 67–76, 78, 79, 90–91, 164

Budget
  retirement worksheet, 154
  sample, 111–13
Burial requests, 50

Cash machine scams, 254–56
Cemetery requests, 50
Certificates of deposit (CDs), 10, 19, 29, 31, 75, 146
Charitable giving, 157–58, 183, 185
Check and checking account scams, 250–52
Children, 9, 11, 17, 21–22, 134–35, 156–58, 187–89
Closed-end automobile leases, 198–99
Collateral, 218
Commissions, 29, 67, 74–76, 78, 79, 96, 97, 104
Commodities market, 70–71
Con games, 240–68
  cash machine scams, 254–56
  check and checking account scams, 250–52
  credit card scams, 261–64
  financial and brokerage scams, 247–49
  home repair scams, 241–45

identity scams, 264–67
medical and health care scams, 245–47
900-number scams, 252–54
tenants and house partner scams, 256–59
Co-signers, 223
CPAs, 50, 82–83
Credit, 18, 159, 213–29
capacity category, 216–17
character category, 217–18
collateral category, 218
co-signers, 223
credit card and identity theft, 227–29, 261–64
establishing in own name, 215, 219–21
secured credit cards, 222–23
Credit reports, 18, 215–16, 221, 224
Cremation, 42

Debt-to-income ratio, 217
Depression generation, 134–35
Direct deposit, 51
Disability insurance, 107, 139, 161
Divorce decrees, 49
Documents, finding and organizing, 49–50
Driver's licenses, 225–26

Early withdrawals, 147–48
Education, 101, 102, 159
Emergency fund, 108, 109
Enron, 161
Equifax Credit Services, 215, 224
Estate planning, 152–53, 156–58, 173–74, 178
Estate taxes, 37, 45, 51, 143–44, 177–79
Executors, 41, 42, 43, 157
Experian, 215, 224

Family limited partnerships, 46
Fear and panic, 12, 13, 22
Federal Deposit Insurance Corporation (FDIC), 11, 79, 146
Final expenses, 41
Financial advisors, 17–18, 50, 56–61, 67–79, 83, 182
Financial and brokerage scams, 247–49
Financial planning, ten guidelines for, 161–63
Fixed expenses, in budget, 106–7
Fixed-income investments, 145–49
Funerals, 43

Gap insurance, 201
Genealogy report, 54

Gift taxes, 158
Grantor, 44
Grasshoppers, 137
Great Depression, 24, 134
Growth-related investments, 145, 146, 158
Guardians, selection of, 41, 104

Health insurance, 103, 107, 110, 139, 161
High-yield municipal bonds, 28–29
Homeowners/renters insurance, 139, 161, 259
Home repair scams, 241–45
Hourly fees, 75, 76, 78, 79
Housing issues, 187–91
Hybrid (balanced) funds, 109

Identity theft, 227–29, 264–67
In-betweeners, 135–36
Inflation, 130, 131, 142, 161
Inflation Multiplier Table, 168
Installment payments, 18
Insurance, 49, 79–80
automobile, 141, 163
disability, 107, 139, 161
gap, 201
health, 103, 107, 110, 139, 161
homeowners/renters, 139, 161, 259
life, 96–97, 107, 139–43, 161, 177
long-term care, 139, 161
nursing-care, 107
rating companies, 89, 163
umbrella liability, 38–39, 139
worksheet for current, 55
Insurance proceeds, 10, 14, 16, 19
Intensive care unit costs, 183–84
Interest rates, 35, 147–49
Interfamily quarrels, 156–57
Internal management fee, 73
International/world holdings, 149, 150
Investing, ten cardinal rules of, 158–60
Investment performance numbers, 132–33
Invoice price, 204
IRAs, 110, 176
Irrevocable trusts, 46, 52, 180

Junk bonds, 146

Land trusts, 46
Large-cap growth stocks, 149, 150
Leasing automobiles, 196–202
Life expectancy, 2, 161
Life insurance, 96–97, 107, 139–43, 161, 177
Life review, 54
Lifespan, anticipated, 130, 131

Lifestyle, maintaining, 129–33, 162, 178
Life-support systems, 52, 183
Living trusts. *See* Revocable living trusts
Living wills, 52–53, 183–84
Long-term care insurance, 139, 161
Lost-client question, 58–59
Lowballing, 206, 211

Manufacturer's holdback, 204–5
Marriage certificate, 49
Medical and health care scams, 245–47
Mid-cap blend stocks, 149
Mileage, in lease agreements, 199–200
Minimum investment requirements, 57–58
Money Growth Rate Factor Table, 165, 167
Morningstar Mutual Funds, 34, 64, 109, 146, 151
Mortgages, 10, 18, 97, 104
Mutual funds, 28, 31, 34, 64, 73, 80–81, 109, 162

Needs and goals, defining, 9, 11, 20
900-number scams, 252–54
No-load investments, 77
Nonfixed expenses, in budget, 107–8
Nursing-care insurance, 107
Nursing home care, 178–79

Obituaries, 14, 19
One-price operations, 209
Open-end automobile leases, 198–99
Organ donor instructions, 50

Pensions, 29, 127, 162
Personal-injury lawsuits, 38
Personal residence trusts, 46
PIN numbers, 254, 255
Portfolio models, basic, 145
Power of attorney, 49, 53–54, 161
Prenuptial agreement, 117–21, 124
Prepaid burial papers, 50
Privacy Rights Clearinghouse, 266
Probate, 37, 43, 45, 46, 175–77
Professional reserve, 94–95
Property taxes, 105, 106
Proprietary funds, avoidance of, 72–74

Remarriage, 28, 110, 116–26
Replacement fund, 106–7
Request-to-switch letter, 79

Residual value, 197
Retirement, 49, 130, 136–38
  budget worksheet, 154
  income worksheet, 155
Revocable living trusts, 33, 37–38, 43–47, 49, 51–53, 103, 111, 160, 179–82, 184–85
Roth Account, 108, 174

Safety deposit boxes, 42, 50
Scams. *See* Con games
Secured credit cards, 222–23
Securities Investor Protection Corporation (SIPC), 79–80
Series 7 registration, 56–57
Single-premium, tax-deferred annuities, 34–35
Small-cap value stocks, 149, 150
Social Security, 29, 130, 162
Stock portfolio, 27–33
Successor trustee, 44, 45, 181–82
Surrender charges, 77, 79, 87, 139
Surrender time, annuity, 36

Tax-deferred annuities, 34–35, 138
Taxes, 34–35, 49, 138, 162, 230–39, 250–52
  audits, 234–38
  estate taxes, 37, 45, 51, 143–44, 177–79
  filing date and place, 235–36
  gift, 158
  guidelines for filing, 234–35
  property, 105, 106
Tenants and house partner scams, 256–59
Term life insurance, 97, 103, 140–41
Three month breathing period, 10, 18–20, 187, 190
Titles, 49
Trade-ins, 206–7
Trans Union, 215, 224
Treasury bonds, 20, 146–49
Trustee, 44, 181

Umbrella liability insurance, 38–39, 139
Unsecured credit cards, 222, 223
Utility bills, 18

Variable annuities, 34–35, 76–77

Warranties, automobile, 200
Whole-life insurance, 96–97, 140
Wills, 40–43, 46, 48, 160, 174, 175. *See also* Estate planning